40 year___ ___

The images of double-deckers on the covers of this *Buses Yearbook* and its counterpart of 40 years ago, *Buses Annual* for 1986, show how much has changed over that period.

The illustration for 1986 was of a Crosville Bristol VRT in Liverpool. A British-built double-decker in the corporate livery of the state-owned National Bus Company, supplemented by the logo of Merseyside PTE, the public authority that specified service levels in that city region. A make and model found in most parts of England and Wales.

It symbolised the status quo. There was not a hint of the seismic change that was about to turn the known world of bus operation upside down, inside out and every other which way into the bargain. Deregulation in October 1986 and privatisation that began around the same time altered practically everything.

Crosville was split in two, sold to separate buyers, parts of it were dismembered into even smaller parts and eventually ceased to exist by that name. Merseyside, and the other six PTEs, lost their powers to coordinate bus services and were obliged to establish arm's length companies to run the ones they operated directly.

Leyland had already closed the Bristol bus factory and soon shut Eastern Coach Works, which built the body on that Crosville VRT. Volvo bought what was left of Britain's biggest bus builder in 1988 and axed most of its products within five years.

Double-deckers ceased to be the universal tools of the trade, as operators discovered how minibuses and small single-deckers could deliver a different sort of service.

The Optare Metrodecker on this year's cover, in the Diamond North West fleet, is a product of those times of huge change. A rare vehicle, built in Britain by a business founded in 1985 to take over one of Leyland's redundant factories and owned latterly by an Indian business that once was a Leyland subsidiary. Operated by one of the smaller of the private sector groups that provide most bus services today.

Among other topics, this *Buses Yearbook* tells the story of the rise and ultimate fall of Optare and of how deregulation and privatisation affected Merseyside and South Yorkshire.

There are a few links with the 1986 edition. Editor Gavin Booth (that was the last of the 15 editions he compiled) and his successor Stewart J Brown made a bus ride (ten in fact) across the north of England from Hull to New Brighton in search of urban authenticity. This year, Bob Hind has taken himself around Dorset in seven buses in search of Thomas Hardy.

A 1986 photo feature about buses in garages included an East Yorkshire open-topper in London for Derby Day, the subject of one of this year's features. And a bus glimpsed in this year's selection at Epsom Downs — an ex-Devon General Atlantean on loan to Hastings & District — was shown in its entirety in a 1986 article on the recently created Hastings company.

There also are familiar names from 1986 among this year's authors — Gavin Booth, Peter Rowlands and Michael Dryhurst although very sadly this is Michael's last, written a short time before his death in September 2025. Peter once again has also worked wonders in digitally enhancing the quality of photographs in several of the articles. ∎

Alan Millar

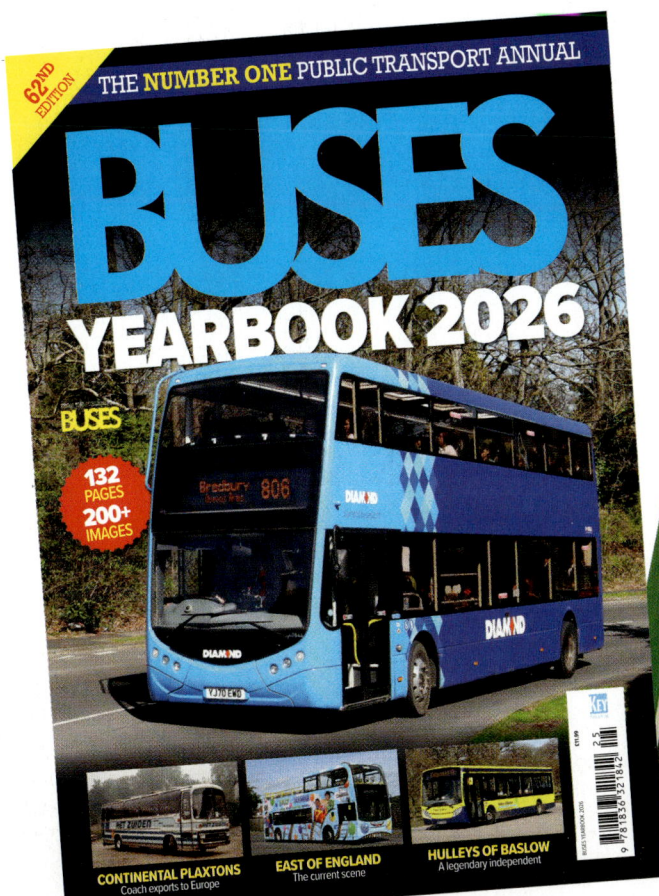

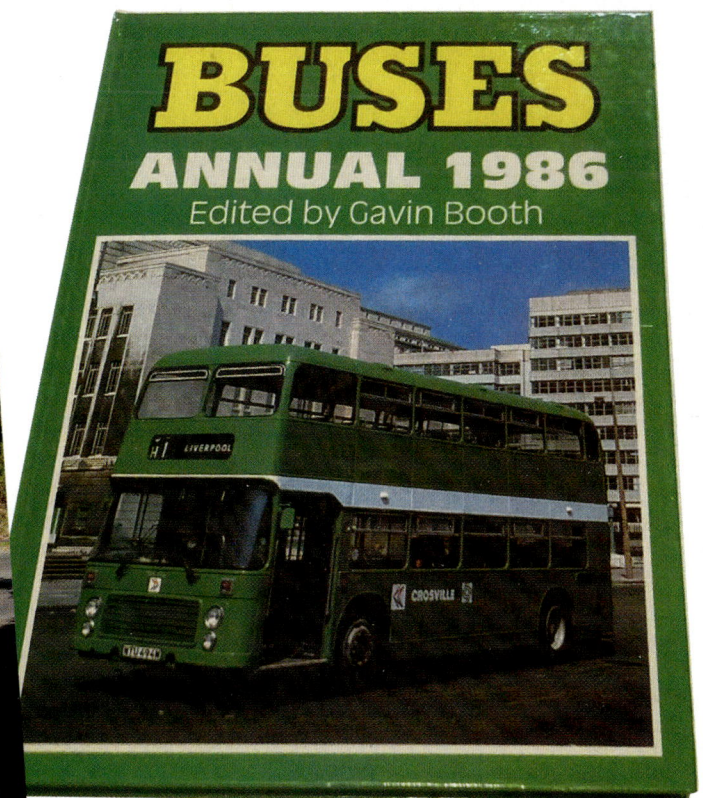

Alexander (Northern) NLO11 (SSA 11X), a Leyland Olympian with Alexander RL-type body, in Dundee in May 1982. See David Toy's article about the Scottish Bus Group's 1980s vehicle purchases on p68. IAIN MACGREGOR

CONTENTS

20

64

92

BUSES

YEARBOOK 2026

ISBN: 978 1 83632 184 2
Editor: Alan Millar
Senior editor, specials: Roger Mortimer
Email: roger.mortimer@keypublishing.com
Senior editor, this edition: Paul Sander
Design: Panda Media

ADVERTISING
Advertising Sales Manager: Sam Clark
Email: sam.clark@keypublishing.com
Tel: 01780 755131
Advertising Production: Becky Antoniades
Email: Rebecca.antoniades@keypublishing.com

SUBSCRIPTION/MAIL ORDER
Key Publishing Ltd, PO Box 300,
Stamford, Lincs, PE9 1NA
Tel: 01780 480404
Subscriptions email: subs@keypublishing.com
Mail Order email: orders@keypublishing.com
Website: www.keypublishing.com/shop

PUBLISHING
Group CEO: Adrian Cox
Publisher: Steve O'Hara

Published by
Key Publishing Ltd, PO Box 100, Stamford,
Lincs, PE9 1XQ
Tel: 01780 755131
Website: www.keypublishing.com

PRINTING
Precision Colour Printing Ltd, Haldane,
Halesfield 1, Telford, Shropshire. TF7 4QQ

DISTRIBUTION
Seymour Distribution Ltd, 2 Poultry Avenue,
London, EC1A 9PU
Enquiries Line: 02074 294000.
We are unable to guarantee the bona fides of
any of our advertisers. Readers are strongly
recommended to take their own precautions
before parting with any information or item
of value, including, but not limited to money,
manuscripts, photographs, or personal
information in response to any advertisements
within this publication.

FRONT COVER: *Diamond North West 40844
(YJ70 EWD), a rare diesel-engined Optare
Metrodecker. The Optare story starts on p6.*
JOHN YOUNG

www.keybuses.com

KEY Publishing

Early Optare products included three coach-seated bodies to Roe design on Leyland Olympians for Cambus, a privatised National Bus Company subsidiary, in February 1988. OPTARE

It opted for Optare

Optare took over an empty factory from Leyland in 1985 and survived through changes of ownership for 40 years, earning a reputation for style and innovation that helped it become the UK's third largest bus builder. **ALAN MILLAR** tells its story.

When Leyland Bus closed its Charles H Roe factory in September 1984, that could have been the end of 41 years of skilled coachbuilding at the Crossgates works in Leeds.

Demand for new buses was plummeting, Leyland was competing with other domestic manufacturers and continental European manufacturers for such business, and Margaret Thatcher's Conservative government was preparing to privatise and deregulate the bus industry, and to sell its majority shareholding in British Leyland.

Leyland had expanded bus production capacity in 1971, by a theoretical 2,000 vehicles a year, opening the Lillyhall plant near Workington to build the single-deck Leyland National. High demand for double-deckers and limited export sales for the National kept its factories open through the 1970s, but that could be sustained no longer.

Bus and truck plants were closed and Leyland's focus moved to north-west England. It shut AEC at Southall

in 1980, Park Royal also in London in 1981, Guy at Wolverhampton in 1982. After Roe closed, Bathgate in West Lothian, a truck plant that produced the Cub bus, went in 1986, Eastern Coach Works (ECW) at Lowestoft in 1987. Volvo acquired Leyland Bus in 1988 and closed Workington in 1993.

Roe was the smallest of Leyland's three remaining bodybuilding plants. Between 1981 and 1983, it produced 368 vehicles, mostly double-deck, against 1,213 (also mainly double-deck) at ECW and 1,155 (increasingly double-deck) at Workington. Roe's total in 1983 was just 93. Output improved over its final nine months, with 91 Olympian double-deckers for West Yorkshire PTE, Bristol Omnibus and London Country, plus 24 Royal Tiger Doyen integral coaches.

Many of Roe's workers wanted to keep the factory open, and garnered political support from West Yorkshire Metropolitan County Council, whose West Yorkshire

Russell Richardson launching the CityPacer in 1986.

Enterprise Board acquired the factory. Rather than promote a worker cooperative, a model with a poor survival record, it sought something more sustainable and made the masterful choice of a former Roe plant director, 36-year-old Russell Richardson, to head the company that leased the Crossgates factory and reopened it in February 1985. He had latterly been plant director at Duple's Blackpool site.

Former employees were required to buy shares in the business, one that needed a name. As an off-the-shelf entity, it was Simco No.49 Ltd, and for 16 days in January 1985 it was Orion of Leeds, but from late March that year it was Optare, Latin for 'to opt for'. While outsiders with a classical education tried to pronounce it 'Op-tar-ay', the company called itself 'Opt-air'.

It dared to be different

Besides a name, Optare needed orders. Quickly. Leyland had sold the building but kept most of its contents and retained the rights to Roe's products. The PTEs of South and West Yorkshire placed early orders for midibus bodies on Dennis Domino (SYPTE) and Leyland Cub (WYPTE) chassis. Optare also built Roe-style double-deck bodies on Olympians for WYPTE and other operators, some under subcontract to Leyland. There also were patient transport ambulances, mobile libraries and, for WYPTE, Freight Rover Sherpa minibus van conversions.

That got things started, but what stopped Optare becoming a nine-day wonder was its desire to be different, not to confine itself to functionary products and to tailor its offer to operators' changing needs.

The greatest changing need was minibuses, which had become flavour of the month. They were cheap to buy, maintain and fuel. Also easy to drive, potentially cheaper to staff and could negotiate residential roads with on-street parking. They helped operators provide higher frequency routes that took passengers closer to their front doors, rivalling taxis.

West Yorkshire's Sherpas were part of that movement, but they were not what Richardson wanted as Optare's signature dishes. By profession he was an engineer, but instinctively also a marketeer, and he spearheaded research into minibus strengths and weaknesses to design a superior product.

Blackpool Transport bought 31 CityPacers in 1987/88.
TERRY BLACKMAN

Northumbria bought 17 Delta-bodied DAF SB220s. The first of them has been restored to original condition.

The strengths were known, but it was not for nothing that the Ford Transit, Mercedes-Benz L608D, Iveco Daily and Sherpa conversions were nicknamed 'bread vans'. They looked no more than that. Passenger accommodation was cramped, they needed more than their 16 to 20 seats and the driving position was too low.

The bus that Optare launched in the summer of 1986 had a coachbuilt body wide enough to accommodate 25 seats in conventional 2+2 fashion, with a raised driving position providing better forward vision and eye contact with passengers. All this on a 5.5tonne Volkswagen LT chassis, a heavier version of a van well established in the UK.

The body was styled with help from art students in Leeds, its large sloping windscreen making it look more like a large car, certainly not a van transporting baked goods. It looked desirable and came with a catchy name, CityPacer, the first of several Optare products identified by a 'camel' word with a hump-like capital letter in the middle.

Although the chassis was from one of the world's largest automotive companies with a widely recognised brand identity, Optare's name drove sales of the CityPacer and most products that followed it.

Early orders came from London and, as operators demanded more than 25 seats, Optare announced the StarRider in 1987, a bigger version on the Mercedes-Benz 811D. There also was an economy version from 1990 that retained the Mercedes bonnet but it only sold four. Optare customers preferred style. That StarRider variant was badged in car fashion as the SRe. We would see similar model identification in the future.

The range develops

Another changing operator need was for large single-deckers, which were being favoured over more expensive double-deckers in the years in the late 1980s, with operators' choice limited to the Leyland Lynx, Volvo B10M, Scania K92 or N112. This was Optare's next opportunity to be different.

It struck an exclusive chassis deal with DAF which, although active with coaches, had yet to enter the UK bus market. Its new SB220 ticked several boxes on operators' wish lists. Like the Lynx, it had a horizontal rear engine, allowing for a lower floor ahead of the rear axle (proper low-floor buses had yet to come) and that engine was the Dutch manufacturer's superior development of the familiar Leyland 680.

The 11.8m Optare body, launched in 1988 and named Delta (D for DAF?), came with Optare's hallmark raked windscreen. It used the Alusuisse bolted aluminium construction system, for which Optare became a UK licensee (as also did Wrights of Ballymena), allowing for more precise assembly and ease of accident repair.

Production began in 1989 — early customers included Go-Ahead Northern, United Auto and Reading Buses — and, as with the CityPacer, the market regarded it as an Optare product that happened to have DAF underpinning. A shorter version announced in 1990 was built on the MAN 11.180 and called the Vecta; it had an upright version of the Delta's windscreen.

More chassis partnerships followed, but Optare took its first step into manufacturing complete vehicles in July 1989, when it acquired the assets, rights and intellectual property of Metro-Cammell Weymann (MCW) from the Laird Group, which was selling its road and rail vehicle businesses. Optare saw potential in the Metrobus double-decker and Metrorider mini/midibus.

The Metrorider, which had a hint of the CityPacer's shape, was a purpose-designed integral bus, typically with 25 seats or 33 seats. It had a front-mounted Cummins or Perkins engine and a choice of automatic (usually Allison) or manual gearbox. It was announced in October 1986 and in production early in 1987.

By the time it closed its Birmingham factory, MCW had sold over 1,000 to an impressive range of operators, but lost money making them and there were issues with build quality, especially body corrosion.

Optare transferred production to Leeds and rationalised the range, dropping the Perkins engine and manual gearbox options, and corrected the build quality weaknesses, especially body leaks and corrosion. It

A MetroRider for Warrington Borough Transport. MIKE THOMSON

One of the first low-floor Spectra-bodied DAF DB250s, new to National Express Group-owned Travel Dundee in early 1998, with later owner Midland Classic.

satisfied itself with smaller volumes, selling more than 1,100 by the time production ended early in 2000. Besides badging it as an Optare with minor styling changes, Metrorider became MetroRider — a camel word for a Metro-Cammell design.

The initial sale of a bus is only the start of a relationship between manufacturer and operator. There is money to earn from supplying replacement parts, especially mechanical ones. As a complete vehicle, the MetroRider gave Optare access to the income which still went to the chassis suppliers on its other products. Here was an incentive to build more integrals.

Optare goes Dutch

Its ability to do so was accelerated in May 1990 when, not for the last time in its 40-year history, Optare found a new owner.

An 11.8m Excel new to Munro's of Jedburgh in 2004.

United Bus, a Dutch venture formed by the November 1989 merger of DAF Bus and Bova, bought Optare for around £5million (equivalent of £13million in 2025).

This enabled Optare to make more changes to the Metrobus than it had when turning the Metrorider into the MetroRider. DAF's chassis engineering left little unaltered than the air suspension and part of the back axle when the chassis was ready for launch in 1991 as the DB250. Optare's Alusuisse body, with hints of the Delta but without a sloped front, was named Spectra. A Greek theme was unfolding with model names. There also was a Turkish connection, as DAF secured an order from the cities of Istanbul and Izmir for 31 left-hand-drive Spectras.

Unfortunately, United Bus was not long for this world. DAF and Leyland had merged their truck businesses in 1987, but the venture collapsed in 1993. United Bus filed for bankruptcy soon after. Most of its constituent parts were sold separately, and Russell Richardson led a management buyout that reacquired Optare, despite a competing bid from the Cowie group whose Hughes DAF dealership was DAF's UK importer.

Hughes DAF had been offering Hungarian-built Ikarus bodies on the SB220 since 1990 and provided additional competition for Optare from late 1994 in a tie-up with Northern Counties to body the SB220 and DB250.

The United Bus collapse led Trent Barton, another early customer for the Delta, to play safe in 1993/94 and order Northern Counties-bodied Volvo B10Bs, and with supply of the SB220 looking less secure, Optare found two other chassis to put under the Delta body structure. The 11.6m Sigma, with the Vecta's upright profile, was launched in 1994 on the Dennis Lance, while the Prisma, launched the next year, was on the 11.8m Mercedes-Benz O405 and

An example of the longest Solo produced, the 10.2m 37-seater, supplied to Brylaine Travel in Boston.

came with the chassis maker's front dash and windscreen, so lacked an Optare look. Volumes of both were small: 54 Sigmas mainly for Go-Ahead Northern, Trent Barton and Brighton & Hove; 122 Prismas mainly for Tees & District, GRT Bus Group and East Yorkshire.

The relationship with DAF endured. The Delta was built until 1998 and a low-floor Spectra, on re-engineered DB250 chassis, was launched in 1997 and produced until 2003.

Lightweight integrals

Optare's growth came with a range of rear-engined lightweight low-floor integrals along the principles established with the MetroRider, with a steel framework in a variety of lengths and with the large windscreens that had been a feature since the CityPacer appeared.

One clever bit was to construct most of the vehicle before installing the engine, gearbox and axles — the most expensive parts — and for these to be easily removable for major service or repair. Fleets and service centres could hold a spare engine ready to be swapped for one requiring attention, keeping the bus in service for longer, earning revenue. It also assisted Optare's cashflow.

The first of these was the Excel, announced in 1995 and produced from 1996, available in four lengths from 9.6m to 11.5m, with a similar Cummins/Allison driveline to the MetroRider. A longer wheelbase Excel 2 launched four years later had the added option of a Mercedes-Benz engine. It was light but had large dimension wheels. Nearly 600 were produced, the last entering service in 2004.

Its successor, the Tempo, was produced from early 2005, with revised body styling and the further options of MAN engine and ZF transmission. It used the same structure as the Excel, but with a redesigned front, and came in four lengths from 10.6m to 12.6m. Production tailed off after 2012 although the last entered service five years later, with around 240 produced.

The second of the new range, the product that sustained Optare for the rest of its existence, was its low-floor, rear-engined successor to the MetroRider, with entrance directly behind the front wheels. The Solo, its name signifying that its entrance step was 'so low', was the first and consistently most successful bus in its class.

Most fleets of any consequence had Solos even if they bought no other Optare product. It was the antithesis of the Henry Ford claim about the Ford Model T — 'You can have it in any colour as long as it's black' — as there were near infinite permutations of length and width, driveline, interior and exterior trim. It was announced in 1997, produced from 1998, and over the 27 years clocked up sales of around 5,900.

Originally available in 8.5m and 9.2m lengths, in one width of 2.5m and powered by a four-cylinder Mercedes-Benz engine, the length options eventually extended from 7.1m to 10.2m, a 2.3m SlimLine width was added and at various stages there were Cummins and MAN engine options.

The restyled Solo SR was announced in 2007 and produced from 2008, initially as an option before becoming the standard model during 2012. The heavily restyled Tempo SR was produced for Trent Barton, which took 14 in 2012; another 22 followed later for Australia, two of which remained in the UK at Manchester Airport.

Front and rear views of two Versas operated by Perryman's Buses, based in Berwick-upon-Tweed.

A Tempo SR, new to Trent Barton, with later owner Ipswich Buses. RICHARD GODFREY

As it was much cheaper to alter the length than engineer a narrower structure, the 10.2m Solo with up to 37 seats was available before the SlimLine models, but there were limits to the practicality of a long wheel forward vehicle that, in old money, was 33ft 5in long. So Optare developed a shorter wheelbase door forward version of the Solo, the Versa, announced in 2006 and produced between 2007 and 2018. It came in lengths between 9.7m and 12.1m, with over 880 built, greatly limiting demand for the Tempo.

The sweeping Solo front gave the Versa a long overhang, making it impractical for London. Optare introduced a derivative in 2013 with a shorter, upright front, the MetroCity, later re-spelt Metrocity after another manufacturer complained that Optare's camel-word model names could be confused with its similar ones. Nearly 300 were produced by 2020, most for use outside London.

Along with these successes was the bus Optare would prefer to forget. It identified community transport as an opportunity for growth. Just like the mainstream bus industry in 1985, this was dominated by converted vans, in this application equipped with powered wheelchair lifts in the back, an arrangement that limits the independence of disabled passengers, is undignified and less safe than kerbside boarding.

Optare's offer was a 16-seat, 7.25m long, 2.08m wide, front-wheel drive low-floor minibus in a car-like composite body, with a wide doorway behind the front wheels, powered by an Iveco engine mated to either a manual or automatic gearbox. This was the Alero, also the name of an Oldsmobile car in North America but not sold in Europe.

It was launched in 2001 with a confident prediction that it would sell 500 a year, doubling the company's output. It was built in Optare's second factory in Rotherham,

A Metrocity demonstrator equipped with the Allison xFE gearbox.

An Alero operating for Stagecoach in Aberdeen in 2006. BOB McGILLIVRAY

The prototype of the double-decker that became the Metrodecker, with Olympus body built at the former East Lancs factory in Blackburn.

acquired in 1996 with the Autobus business, a bodybuilder of light truck-derived minicoaches that complemented its presence in the bus market. Its confidence was misplaced. Community transport providers preferred the simplicity and reliability of cheaper mass-produced vans and barely 300 Aleros were built when deliveries ended in 2008.

Four more owners

All this occurred against the background of successive changes of ownership. NABI, short for North American Bus Industries, acquired Optare in January 2000 for around £21million. Despite its name, NABI was Hungarian, assembling buses in Alabama for United States transit fleets. When founded in 1992 it was called American Ikarus and had grown out of the same Ikarus business in Hungary that supplied bodies to Hughes DAF to compete with the Optare Delta, and which had supplied the Soviet Bloc before the Iron Curtain fell.

NABI had developed a one-piece composites body, branded CompoBus, to produce lighter US transit buses, technology that Optare could draw on with the Alero. A left-hand-drive Solo was developed for the US market, badged as a NABI, and a high-floor version of the Excel body, on a Scania chassis, was sold in Hungary.

NABI ownership ended in 2005 when Optare's management, led by managing director Bob Coombes, who had previously been with Dennis, bought the company back for £11.8million. Russell Richardson, latterly non-executive chairman, stepped down but continued to assist in a consultancy capacity.

Optare had another new owner in March 2008. The buyer was Jamesstan Investments, controlled by Roy

Stanley, chairman of the Alternative Investment Market (AIM)-listed Tanfield Group whose other businesses included Smith Electric Vehicles. Another of Stanley's businesses, Darwen Group, acquired East Lancashire Coachbuilders out of administration in 2007. He and colleagues had tried to buy Plaxton from its management buyout team that year, but it instead became part of Alexander Dennis.

Optare had considered acquiring East Lancs in the early 1990s. Now it was being taken over by the Blackburn company's latest owner. The two companies were merged in July 2008, with Darwen renamed Optare and listed on AIM. East Lancs double- and single-deck bodies were rebranded as Optare and a plan was announced to relocate production in a large new factory in Blackburn, to be supported by a smaller one in Leeds. Tempo production moved to the former East Lancs factory.

The new Optare went to the Euro Bus Expo show in Birmingham in November 2008 with one of the biggest stands on which, among other things (of which more later), was a redesigned Solo, the Solo+. Given that the Solo SR was announced only a year earlier, this was a surprise and its bland looks earned it no favours. The two at the show, the only ones built, were turned into standard Solos soon after.

Chief executive Andrew Brian resigned a month after the show, the new Blackburn factory project was dropped, and the planned closure of the Rotherham site was delayed until later in 2009.

Stability began to return from June that year with the appointment of former Leyland Trucks managing director Jim Sumner as Optare's chief executive. Russell

Richardson, who had made public after the 2008 takeover that he had ceased to be involved with the business, once again provided advice and assistance.

The business needed to be restored to profit, and Sumner knew it also needed a strategic partner to invest in Optare's future. That emerged in mid-2010 as Ashok Leyland, part of the Indian-owned Hinduja Group and a one-time Leyland subsidiary. Two major export orders were secured for the Solo, one from South Africa for 190 assembled locally for Cape Town in 2012/13, the other from Dubai for 94 left-hand-drive models in 2019.

A new factory at Sherburn-in-Elmet, just over the North Yorkshire boundary, replaced the Leeds and Blackburn factories in 2011; the East Lancs-designed Olympus and Visionaire double-deck bodies died with the Blackburn closure.

Quest for a double-decker

Optare finally reached its long-promised goal of having an integral double-decker when it launched the MetroDecker, later re-spelt Metrodecker, in May 2014. It talked of such a vehicle when the NABI takeover was announced and accompanied the Solo+ exhibits at the 2008 exhibition with a double-decker called Rapta, which visitors suspected was a full-size mock-up.

In 2011 it unveiled a prototype, with Olympus body on an underframe with a Mercedes-Benz engine, that had been on test for several months and exported it later to Malta,

converted to open-top. The Metrodecker had a lightweight steel structure like that of the integral single-deckers. Its styling was restrained by Optare's past standard.

Between 2010 and 2018, Ashok Leyland increased its shareholding from 26% to 99% and in November 2020 renamed the company Switch Mobility, a brand it intended to use solely on electric buses. Diesel buses would still be badged Optare.

Optare had unveiled a battery-powered Solo in 2009, and the low weight of its body structures suited heavy battery electric technology. The Solo, Versa and Metrocity all became available with electric drive, and 109 of the 118 Metrodeckers built were electric (mainly for London and York), although production only began in 2019 and ended two years later, beset by slow delivery. The only order for the diesel version, from Reading Buses for five, was cancelled pre-delivery; other buyers were found for them.

Production of diesel Solos appeared to end in 2022 but resumed in 2024 with an order for 118 from Stagecoach, a customer since 2001. A further 17 were built for other operators. The last one went to Ross Travel of Featherstone in August 2025, appropriately a Yorkshire company that bought 13 Solos over the previous 20 years.

And that was the end of Optare as we knew it. Switch Mobility announced in March 2025 that the Sherburn factory would close and its surplus assets, including part built and prototype vehicles, were sold four months later. It had been good while it lasted. ■

Solo SRs, mainly left-hand-drive models for Dubai, and Metrodeckers for London in the Sherburn-in-Elmet factory in March 2019.

Left-hook Plaxtons

Although most of its coach production has been for domestic customers, Plaxton's Scarborough factories have also built bodies for continental European operators. **MIKE FENTON** was in the right places at the right times to photograph several of these, as well as a former British midibus exported in later life.

In the aftermath of World War Two, with Britain all but bankrupt, vehicle manufacturers were encouraged to export to earn foreign currency. One that took this to heart was Seddon Motors of Oldham, builders in 1948 of a couple of left-hand-drive Mark 4 chassis that were bodied by Plaxton and exported to the Portuguese island of Madeira and the SAM (Sociedade de Automóveis da Madeira) fleet of Funchal, the island capital. When new, the vehicle shown was registered M-2773, with its entrance at the rear. However, in 1955, in keeping with all other Madeiran vehicles, it was re-registered in a new series, becoming MA-23-86 and then at some point rebuilt to forward entrance, as seen in Funchal in September 1978.

It was in 1976 when Plaxton began building coach bodies on DAF chassis for operators in the Netherlands. First out of the blocks in May were two 11m rear-engined SB1602 with 50-seat Supreme bodies for Meering Touringcars of Duivendrecht, near Amsterdam. The next, 94-84-TB, in January 1977, was unique in having an 8.5m 29-seat Supreme body on an FA1100 chassis. It was new to Gebo Tours of Nijverdal, but by April 1981 was with Ezaco Reizen of Haarlem.

A further 16 Supreme-bodied DAF SB1602 50-seaters followed for Netherlands operators in 1977, along with two 12m SB1605s with 50-seat Viewmaster bodies. One of the latter was 81-AB-12, new in December 1977 to Spauwen of Valkenburg, in the southern province of Limburg, photographed in July 1978. The fleetname Het Zuiden translates as The South.

Typifying later Plaxton-bodied DAFs for the Netherlands was 40-TB-85, shot in April 1981 at the Keukenhof Gardens bulb fields 20miles south-west of Amsterdam. It was new in April 1980 to Oostenrijk Touringcars of Diemen, near Amsterdam, and one of an eventual total of 21 with 11.9m Supreme IV bodies on DAF SB2005 chassis. To comply with Dutch turning circle legislation, this and the others had bodies tapering in at the front and, as a result, narrower than normal windscreens.

Plaxton also built bodies for Danish operators from 1975, but on a far greater range of chassis. The earliest of these was BN 98 636; a 53-seat Supreme body on a 12m rear-engined Magirus Deutz of 230 R120 type. Its owner from new in July 1975 was Leif Nielsen of Strøby, co-owner of Plaxton importer A/S Magnabus, but had passed to V Nymand of Nykøbing, 40miles north-west of Copenhagen, when photographed in September 1979.

Another notable Supreme for Denmark was this 12m Volvo B755-08 rebody operated by Auto Paaske of Copenhagen. The horizontal underfloor-engined chassis was new in December 1964 to Forenede Rutebiler of Søborg, near Copenhagen, registered KA 78 234, with a 31-seat three-door Nordisk Karosserifabrik standee bus body. Plaxton rebodied it as a 58-seat coach, in which condition it re-entered service in January 1976, re-registered CB 99 312.

16

Plaxton bodied 48 Ford R1114 chassis for Denmark between 1975 and 1977, with this one, BZ 98 862, a 53-seater new in August 1976 to Nordfalsters Turistfart of Vordingborg on the island of Zealand. Besides these 11 Fords, it also supplied Danish operators with 45-seat 10m bodies on nine R1014 chassis in 1977.

Eleven forward-entrance Supreme bodies on wheel-forward Bedford VAS5 chassis were supplied to Denmark, six in 1976 and five in 1977, with seating capacities ranging from 25 to 30. The owner of EB 97 716, a 28-seater, was Jørgen Pedersen of Sandager, on the island of Funen.

The exports to Denmark also included 40 Bedford YMTs, 35 of them to the usual length of 11m. Nine had chassis shortened to 10m and six on chassis extended to 12m. EV 93 559, with a 49-seat Supreme body, was new in May 1979 to Ruteautomobil Aktieselskabet of Haderslev in the south of Jutland, not far from the border with Germany.

Plaxton teamed up with Volvo in 1992 to offer the Prestige 370, a 3.7m high version of the Excalibur body, on the left-hand-drive, rear-engined B12 chassis. It was intended primarily for the French market, but fewer than 20 were built, some of which went to operators in Italy. At least three of the French examples were 53-seaters operated by Autocar Redon Tourisme of Vitry-sur-Seine, Paris. This April 1996 photograph shows one of these, 5542 SK 93, crossing the River Seine via the Pont de la Tournelle, a short distance upstream from the Île de la Cité and Notre Dame.

Plaxton-bodied coaches in Estonia may well have been limited to just this DAF SB3000 with a 50-seat Paramount III 3500 body, photographed in the Baltic state's capital in August 2006 with Omnibuss Tallinn. It was new in May 1987 to Netherlands operator Snelle Vliet of Hardinxveld, registered BK-28-KK, then in 1996 exported to Estonia where it ran as 079 AKP until 2008.

This selection ends as it began, with a Plaxton bus-bodied vehicle, but not one exported from new. With the proliferation of low-floor single-deckers in the UK, many step-entrance midibuses were withdrawn prematurely and several were sold for use abroad. Among them was R165 ESG, a 29-seat Beaver 2-bodied Mercedes-Benz Vario O814D new in August 1997 to Travel Bell of Silksworth. It went to Poland, converted to left-hand-drive and registered KTA 5626A. When photographed in May 2012, in Tarnów, 45miles east of Kraków, it was still in the livery of its previous owner, Vale of Manchester.

The 1956 ground-breaking Leyland/MCW Atlantean integral prototype, 281 ATC, presented a more striking appearance than the early production versions. GAVIN BOOTH COLLECTION

Dedicated followers of fashion

GAVIN BOOTH considers how the layout and appearance of the double-decker changed over 40 years after Leyland and AEC produced new models in 1954

t is 1954. Two teams of engineers and designers, more than 200miles apart, are busy working on the next generation of double-deck buses. In south-east England, London Transport has earned a well-deserved reputation for producing useful and attractive buses for its own vast network. In Lancashire, Leyland has catered for mainstream demand from customers in the UK and abroad and has defied convention with some ground-breaking models.

The London team is working on a motorbus to replace its trolleybuses, that would emerge later in 1954 as the Routemaster, a stylish and technically advanced front-engined design with an open rear platform that represented the ultimate expression of this very British icon. Between

1954 and 1968, 2,760 would be built for London Transport use, plus 65 for British European Airways (BEA) services and 50 for Northern General – plus one rear-engined prototype.

The BEA and Northern General buses, and one of London Transport's, had forward entrances. The Routemaster proved to be very successful and popular where it was operated, with the last examples still running in normal service in 2005.

Leyland was working on a model that would render the Routemaster and its ilk obsolete – the rear-engined Atlantean. There had been a few rear-engined Leylands before, and two experimental double-deckers were assembled in 1953/54, but a fortuitous change in the

Prototype Daimler Fleetline CRD6 (Daimler engine) 7000 HP of 1960 carried a plain 77-seat Metro-Cammell body, slightly relieved by the fluted Daimler logo on the front panel. GAVIN BOOTH COLLECTION

regulations governing vehicle lengths in 1956 permitting 30ft long double-deckers allowed Leyland to create the template for what would become tens of thousands of double-deckers from a range of manufacturers.

The prototype Atlantean was unveiled at the 1956 Commercial Motor Show and was unlike anything we had seen before. It had been designed as a lowheight integral bus with 78-seat Metro-Cammell bodywork with an entrance ahead of the front wheels, like most contemporary single-deckers.

Bury Corporation specified Metro-Cammell's Liverpool design on 15 Atlanteans delivered in 1963. By 1970, what had been its 111 (REN 111) was 6311 in the Selnec PTE fleet. IAIN MacGREGOR

While operators liked the look and concept, they were unhappy that it was an integral, which would prevent them from specifying bodies from their favoured suppliers. So, it was back to the drawing-board to redesign the Atlantean as a less complicated chassis.

At the 1958 Commercial Show four Atlanteans were on display with fairly uninspiring bodies, two by Metro-Cammell, one by Weymann and one by Alexander. These were clearly derived from the big selling Metro-Cammell Orion design fitted to many front-engined double-deckers, its looks much-reviled in some quarters, and lacked the 'wow' factor.

Busiest bodybuilders

In terms of bus chassis output, the great rivals AEC and Leyland ruled the roost in the mid-1950s, and the two busiest bodybuilders were Metro-Cammell and Park Royal. AEC and Park Royal were in common ownership and were about to embark on production of the Routemaster. Leyland had closed its bodybuilding department in 1954 and forged strong links with Metro-Cammell.

Maybe Leyland and the bodybuilders missed a trick. Instead of pushing the boundaries, their designs looked bland and while the mere presence of Atlanteans in these early days initially caused a stir, as large Atlantean fleets became more common, some operators longed for something more eye-catching and worked with bodybuilders to create distinctive body styles that prompted fresh thinking about what might attract more passengers to use buses.

The sizeable municipal operators had the most clout, so Liverpool Corporation worked with Metro-Cammell to

Alexander's J-type body, with panoramic side windows and a nearside staircase, on a preserved 33ft Atlantean PDR2/1 new to Tyneside PTE in 1972.

produce a distinctive design and Glasgow Corporation worked with Alexander to produce a classic and much-imitated style. This was helped by changes in regulations that permitted the use of non-opening one-piece windscreens which in turn encouraged the use of curved glass screens at the front of both decks.

This, coupled with increasing use of glassfibre for the front dash and roof domes, meant that double-deckers could break away from flat panels. While the rest of the body may not have changed much, a facelift made all the difference.

When other operators saw what rear-engined double-deckers could look like, some of them nagged their tame bodybuilders to come up with something more up-to-date. A couple specified the Liverpool design; others went to Alexander or asked their suppliers to create Alexander lookalikes and East Lancs and Weymann obliged. Alexander had also pioneered the use of much longer side windows and there was a brief interest in these, but only Edinburgh stuck to these until 1981 for its large fleet of Atlanteans.

Made-to-measure

East Lancs had built up a reputation for well-built made-to-measure bodies mainly for the municipal sector and was more inclined to bow to the whims of general managers to adapt its basic body style.

Bolton Corporation specified this unique East Lancs body style with sloping window pillars on 15 Atlanteans delivered in 1969/70, just as Selnec PTE took over. IAIN MacGREGOR

The distinctive Mancunian body style was created by Manchester Corporation in 1968. This was the first, a Park Royal-bodied Atlantean preserved at the Museum of Transport Greater Manchester. This body style was also built by East Lancs, MCW and Roe. TONY WILSON

A 1974 Daimler Fleetline of Greater Manchester Transport, with 75-seat Northern Counties body, in Oldham in 1981.

The major players — essentially Metro-Cammell and Park Royal — pursued large orders and if the customer was important enough would tailor bodies to suit local tastes. They could choose from flat glass, curved glass or barrel-shaped windscreens, Alexander-style fronts, curved or peaked front domes – or, presumably, any combination of the above.

The most significant example of an operator breaking new ground was the impressive Mancunian design created by and built for Manchester Corporation in 1968, which continued in build from 1969 for the newly-created Selnec PTE, which had gathered over 2,500 buses from 11 municipal bus fleets in the area around Manchester; these included the fleets at Bolton and Oldham that had already specified attractive designs on their latest double-deckers.

But the new PTE was working on a completely new standard double-deck design, and this first appeared in 1971 on Daimler Fleetline and Leyland Atlantean chassis; these 21 experimental buses with Northern Counties bodies were used throughout the PTE's area and paved the way for 1,700 more broadly similar buses delivered between 1972 and 1984 on Atlantean and Fleetline chassis with bodies by Northern Counties and Park Royal.

The roots of this body style, with four main side windows on the upper deck and a short window over the engine compartment, dated back to 1969 when Park Royal supplied Fleetlines to East Kent Road Car, and other bodybuilders produced their own variations. These were Park Royal's sister company, Roe, as well as Metro-Cammell Weymann (MCW), Northern Counties and Willowbrook. At one stage similar bodies by the different builders were being supplied to London, four of the PTEs and several of the larger National Bus Company fleets.

When London Transport bought its first rear-engined double-deckers in 1965, it bought Atlanteans and

Fleetlines with bodies to a very uninspiring Park Royal design, when Park Royal was already producing more attractive buses for other operators. And when it ordered substantial batches of Fleetlines, the MCW and Park Royal bodies seemed less attractive than the styles previously built for the newly-established PTEs, notably Selnec.

The other main bodybuilders – Alexander, East Lancs and Eastern Coach Works (ECW) – stuck to their own designs. ECW bodies, previously restricted to state-owned companies became generally available in 1965 following a share exchange with Leyland, had been straightforward and attractive, but a couple of customers looking for more eye-catching buses — Sheffield and Colchester corporations — specified peaked rather than rounded front and rear domes.

Competition breaks out

Competitors were waiting to challenge what was seen as Leyland's growing monopoly following a spate of acquisitions in the 1960s, including that of AEC in 1962. MCW initially tried to protect its business in a joint venture with the Swedish builder Scania which produced the Metro-Scania single-decker in 1969, and in 1973 the Metropolitan double-decker, both with air suspension. These were impressive-looking and fast buses, but their lives were cut short by corrosion and gearbox problems.

Leyland improved the Atlantean in 1972 and concentrated its efforts in developing a new double-decker intended to replace the Atlantean, Fleetline and Bristol VRT trio. This first appeared in prototype form in 1975 and was available to buy as the Titan TN15 from 1978.

Although it was a fine bus, it also was a technically complex and expensive design, and only London Transport bought it in any quantity; other operators made it clear that it was not what they wanted. It was conceived as a complete bus but outside London what operators wanted was a simpler bus with bodywork by their preferred suppliers.

Dennis had launched the Dominator chassis in 1977 and MCW had realised that building only bodies for

The National Bus Company bought Park Royal-bodied Leyland Atlanteans of the basic style evolved for Greater Manchester. These two 71-seat London Country 1974 deliveries, from a batch of three that replaced ex-London Transport Atlanteans sold to Hong Kong, were at Chessington Zoo on a private hire when new.

Nottingham City Transport had a unique approach to double-deck body design, bought mainly from East Lancs and Northern Counties. This rare 1983 Dennis Falcon V had an 88-seat East Lancs body.

The styling on the ECW body on this Brighton & Hove Bristol VRT/SL3, new to Southdown in 1977, evolved from designs the coachbuilder mounted on front-engined chassis in the early 1950s, but made more up-to-date by incorporating curved windscreens.

buses was not enough and introduced the Metrobus in 1978. Although it was sold mainly as a complete bus, and won substantial orders from London and the West Midlands it was also offered as an underframe bodied by Alexander and Northern Counties.

These were among a stream of new double-deck models that was now appearing – the front-engined Volvo Ailsa in 1973 and rear engined chassis in the 1980s and early 1990s from Leyland and Scania. Leyland's Olympian became the best seller and in addition to bodies from ECW and Roe, part of the Leyland family, there was the new R-type from Alexander.

Kerb appeal

Deregulation in the mid-1980s brought a sometimes-reluctant acceptance that it is worth paying extra for a bus with kerb appeal, one that looks good alongside today's cars, and that offers passengers an attractive and warm ride with well-spaced seats and stylish upholstery.

Optare, which had taken over the Roe factory from Leyland, quickly established a reputation for stylish bodywork. Its double-deck Spectra on DAF DB250 chassis caused a sensation when it was launched at the 1991 Coach & Bus Show, with its gently rounded front end, creating a look that its longer established competitors sought to emulate.

In 1993 Alexander retaliated with the Royale, a reskinned and more rounded version of the R-type and in the same year Northern Counties introduced its equivalent, the Palatine II. But there were already the first signs of a major design revolution.

Low-floor single-deckers were becoming more common on mainland Europe and in 1993 Neoplan had supplied the first example for a UK operator which opened the floodgates over the next few years. It seemed inevitable that low-floor double-deckers might follow, as indeed they did, but that is another story.

In the 40 years from those first production Atlanteans in 1958, the UK double-deck market had moved decisively to

rear-engined models and bodybuilders had responded to calls for more attractive designs. But the main players had changed.

AEC, Bristol, Daimler, Guy and even Leyland were no longer building chassis, their places taken by a reinvigorated Dennis and by imports, notably Scania and Volvo. On the bodybuilding side ECW, MCW, Park Royal, Roe and Willowbrook were consigned to the history books, while Alexander, East Lancs and Optare survived to fight another day. There must be a moral there somewhere. ■

The Palatine II was Northern Counties' answer to the early 1990s demand for a more stylish front, with curved upper and lower deck windscreens. This was a Dennis Arrow in the Capital Citybus fleet operating a long-term rail replacement service for the East London line, which then was part of the London Underground network.

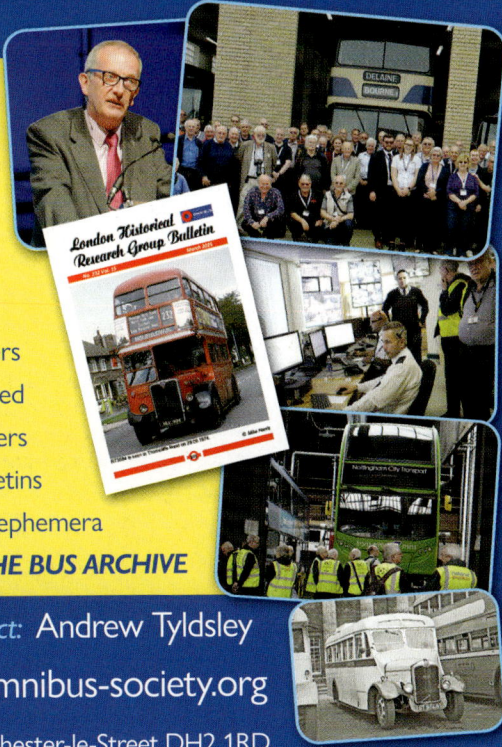

Alexander's A-type body first appeared in Newcastle in the mid-1960s. The multiple-curvature upper front window was the same as the rear window of the bodybuilder's Y-type single-decker. This 1976 photograph, taken in Blackett Street, shows Atlantean ETN 82C in original livery, but with Tyne & Wear PTE logo on the side. Behind it is a Weymann-bodied imitation in later mainly-cream livery.

The sincerest form of flattery

Bus bodybuilders have often imitated each other's styling – sometimes loosely, sometimes almost slavishly. **PETER ROWLANDS** reflects on some striking examples from over the years.

Imagine a car rental company saying to Ford, "We'd like to buy a batch of cars from you, but please make them look like Vauxhalls."

It sounds inconceivable, yet in the bus world this kind of thing was once surprisingly common. Batches of buses were built to order, so a large operator could exercise considerable power in dictating the main features of a given batch, and even what they looked like.

The copies were not always precise, but in the postwar years bigger operators such as London Transport could define exactly what their bodies looked like, and usually the bodybuilders had to comply. Even when there were differences, items such as window glasses were often based on the same standard.

By the 1960s, such instances were less thorough-going but tended to be more interesting as a result. Copycat bodies often looked quite like the bodies they were imitating, but not often exactly like them.

I became aware of this phenomenon when Newcastle Transport started buying Leyland Atlanteans. The first batch to be bodied for the operator by Walter Alexander had unprepossessing flat fronts, but then the coachbuilder developed a much more stylish look using glassfibre mouldings and multiple-curvature front windows on both decks.

Newcastle had a dual-supplier policy, so its other bodybuilder, Weymann, was expected to provide something similar. What it came up with was enough

Two of Tyne & Wear PTE's Weymann-bodied ex-Newcastle Atlanteans with Alexander-lookalike front ends pick up in Grainger Street in 1976. The destination indicators were placed higher than on Alexander bodies, and the air vent in the front dome was an unmistakable identifier.

of an approximation to have confused enthusiasts over the years but was not by any means a copy. The curved windscreens and rounded front dome borrowed unapologetically from the Alexander design, but the body structure and back end were pure Weymann. The lower front mouldings, headlights and destination panel positions and design were also different.

Most strikingly, the Weymann dome featured the company's standard rectangular air vent, which meant Weymann bodies were very easy to distinguish at a glance from their Alexander counterparts.

As the 1960s progressed, other bodybuilders introduced a curving front look, though few followed the Alexander styling as closely as this. One that did was Northern Counties, which used a very similar design for four Leyland Atlanteans bodied for Ashton-under-Lyne Corporation in 1970.

The more typical Northern Counties curving body style of this period had a shallower windscreen based on the standard BET single-decker of the day, and its upper-deck front window had horizontal top and bottom edges, unlike the bowed Alexander variety.

Hints of this body style resurfaced in 1979 in a batch of 30 rather strange 79-seat bodies built by Willowbrook for Tyne & Wear PTE – although the slightly rounder dome disguised the similarities. The unusual six-bay bodywork was built on long-wheelbase Leyland Atlantean chassis, and in its yellow PTE livery this body style was vaguely evocative of the many Alexander-bodied Atlanteans still in the fleet, though to some eyes it probably seemed a rather half-hearted imitation.

Square-cut look

Back in the 1960s, some operators rebelled against the traditional rounded look for their rear-engined double-deckers, hoping to achieve something more square-cut and modern-looking. This gave rise to the strange compromise of peaked front (and usually rear) domes applied to bodywork with curved coving panels.

Liverpool Corporation was a pioneer of this look, working initially with Metro-Cammell; but the approach was adopted with vigour by Alexander, which took it through various iterations during the 1970s; and for a while others followed suit, including East Lancs and Roe.

A more thorough change in the look of double-deckers came in 1968 with the launch of Manchester's

Northern Counties built four of these bodies on Atlantean chassis for Ashton-under-Lyne Corporation in 1970, using a front end closely resembling Weymann's take on the contemporary Alexander design. They were delivered after the organisation was absorbed into Selnec PTE in 1969. VTE 163H is seen in August 1981 at Piccadilly station, Manchester, with a later Northern Counties Manchester standard behind.

A 1977 batch of 30 long-wheelbase Atlanteans for Tyne & Wear PTE were given unusual six-bay Willowbrook bodywork, featuring a front end that some saw as a flattened version of the idiosyncratic Nottingham style of the time. They had two doorways and featured the PTE's then-standard nearside staircase.

Mancunians. Their clean-cut appearance was defined in-house and developed with Park Royal Vehicles, but three other bodybuilders — Metro-Cammell Weymann (MCW), East Lancs and Roe — also built bodies to the same pattern.

Park Royal and MCW followed the Mancunian profile closely in the Daimler Fleetline bodywork they both built for London Transport from 1970 onwards, although the deep windscreen was rejected in favour of the barrel-type curved screen already used on London single-deckers. Later MCW adopted a similar body profile for its Metropolitan, launched in 1973, and for its Metrobus in 1977.

The Mancunian's more extreme features (square corners, deep windscreen) found more muted expression in the Manchester standards that followed the Mancunian in the 1970s. Northern Counties became the primary supplier, but a slightly different Park Royal version was also regarded as part of this standard.

It took Alexander many years to change the face of its double-decker bodywork, but it finally introduced the square-cut R-type body in 1980. This was widely admired and was unrepentantly copied three years later by East Lancs, whose version became known as its E-type. The driving force behind it was South Yorkshire PTE, which wanted the East Lancs bodies on a batch of Dennis Dominators to match existing Alexander bodies in its fleet.

Surprisingly, over the next few years this Alexander copy became virtually a standard offering from East Lancs, being built alongside bodies using the maker's own styling, and it was provided on a variety of chassis makes. Later versions introduced detailing specific to East Lancs, but they all retained the overall Alexander look. South Yorkshire also specified R-type windscreens on Dominators bodied by Northern Counties.

Coach designs

In the world of coaches, arguably the greatest trendsetter was Plaxton's Panorama Elite, launched in 1968. Although other bodybuilders never slavishly copied it, the basic design, with inward-curving sides and distinctive multiple-curvature windscreen, became the pattern that most of its UK-based rivals ended up imitating to a greater or lesser extent.

The most obvious example was Duple's Dominant, which was launched in 1972 and remained available well into the 1980s, later competing with Plaxton's Elite

Echoes of Manchester's square-cornered Mancunians were strongly in evidence in the Daimler Fleetlines bodied by Park Royal and MCW for London Transport in the 1970s. MCW-bodied ex-London KUC 223P was working in Bournemouth for Wilts & Dorset in June 1985.

MCW's Metropolitan, launched in 1973 on Scania running units, picked up the basic Mancunian look, adding asymmetric flair to the windscreen. Newport's GKG 38N is one of ten bought in 1975.

Alexander's ultimately ubiquitous R-type bodywork, launched in 1981, is seen here on 1983 MCW Metrobus BLS 430Y, delivered to Midland Scottish and transferred to the new Kelvin Scottish company in 1985. This is the lowheight RL version.

replacement, the Supreme. Although by no means a copy, it was far more like the Plaxton product range than anything the company had offered before. It was the work of the same designer.

Strong elements of the Elite design can also be seen in the ill-fated Willowbrook 003 body, commissioned by the National Bus Company (NBC), which incorporated the same front and rear windows as its existing Duple Dominants.

Production began in 1979, but the company was unable to handle the work load required by the order for 200-plus bodies, and build quality suffered. The saga nearly brought the company to its knees, and it closed four years later.

East Lancs's copy of Alexander's R-type was convincing, although the multiple-curvature windscreen on Volvo Olympian M640 EPV in the Ipswich fleet has more in common with the arch-topped windscreens of Alexander's previous A-type. It was one of three delivered in 1995.

Plaxton's Panorama Elite of 1968, with its inward-tapered sides, defined British coach styling for almost a generation. This London Country example, on a 1972 AEC Reliance chassis, was new to Barton Transport.

The Duple Dominant coach, launched in 1972, bore an unmistakable resemblance to the Plaxton Elite. This United Counties Leyland Leopard was new in 1977.

Other bodybuilders were also influenced by the Panorama Elite – for instance Eastern Coach Works, which launched its MkII body for the Bristol RE coach chassis in the early 1970s. The overall profile and frontal appearance were strikingly evocative of the Elite, though it had flat rather than curved side window glasses. The design was dropped after a few years but reappeared in modified B51 form in 1982 in a large NBC order, eventually being used on both Leyland Leopard and Tiger chassis.

Walter Alexander was also influenced by the Elite shape. In 1982 it announced a new take on its T-type bus and coach body range, using a profile distinctly reminiscent of the Elite. This was no slavish copy, but the nod to the Plaxton body shape was unmistakable.

Then as late as 1989 East Lancs joined the Elite lookalike trend with its EL2000 body. This was a bus rather than a coach, but the inward-tapered profile and wrap-around windscreen were notably reminiscent of the Dominant coach.

Double-deck coaches

Double-deck coaches have also seen their share of imitation – perhaps never more so than when MCW's double-deck Metroliner was launched in 1983. Although based on the existing tri-axle Metrobus chassis, it had an entirely new body with deep wrap-around front windows on both decks. What struck many observers at the time was the obvious similarity to Belgian manufacturer Van

When ECW launched a redesigned coach body for the rear-engined Bristol RE in the early 1970s, the nod to the Elite design was clear. This Greater Manchester Transport example, delivered to Selnec in 1973, was on a mid-engined Leyland Leopard.

Willowbrook's 003 bodywork was modelled on the Duple Dominant at the request of the National Bus Company. Typical was this Maidstone & District 1983 Leopard.

MCW's Metroliner bore a marked resemblance to Van Hool's Astromega but was much taller. West Midlands Travel acquired three in 1986 through its Central Coachways operation for a short-lived Birmingham-London service run jointly with London Transport.

Hool's well-established Astromega integral.

Like most continental double-deckers, the Astromega was only 4m (13ft) high, whereas the Metroliner was 4.23m (13ft 9in). Nevertheless, the nod to the Astromega's design was unmistakable, especially in the windscreens and bonded side windows.

Eventually the Van Hool/MCW frontal appearance started to influence the look of service buses. The Optare Spectra double-decker, launched in 1991 when Optare was owned by Netherlands-based United Bus, featured broadly similar wrap-around front windows on both decks. The chassis was a development of the original Metrobus design, acquired by United Bus subsidiary DAF Bus when MCW closed in 1989.

Then two years later, Northern Counties launched its Palatine II body, in this case featuring a dramatic extra-deep windscreen reminiscent of the Mancunian's, and Alexander launched its rather similar Royale body. These two designs were both seen as premium alternatives to the makers' existing double-deck bodies.

These days like-for-like copying of individual bus manufacturers' body styles is more or less a thing of the past, but broad similarity between makes of bodywork has become commonplace – driven by the makers' anxiety not to diverge from acknowledged norms, and by the operators' push for commonality of parts.

Whether the bus world is the better for this is a matter of opinion. ■

Van Hool's 4m high Astromega featured distinctive wrap-around front windows on both decks. This Southend Transport example was operating its express service to London.

Typifying the fleet of Global on Gran Canaria is this 15m Castrosua Magnus II-bodied Volvo B12B from a batch of 20 delivered in 2009. JOHN YOUNG

Notes on the high seas

As a jobbing musician, **LAURENCE KNIGHT** struggled for work during the challenging winter months. Then, in 2012 along came the solution which introduced him to strange-sounding places and some strange-looking buses.

The depressing atmosphere of the holiday camp as it closed for the winter was matched by the accommodation – a cold, damp caravan close to a railway line, rattled nightly by freight trains. As I scooped out mould-ridden slippers from under the bed, I ruminated on future work prospects. "North Sea Ferries," said my bass player. "They're desperate for pianists.".

Desperate? Only slightly slighted, I hit the road. My ancient Ford Transit was soon parked among the period police cars at Borehamwood television studios as I auditioned for a life at sea. Not long after, it was chugging north through the early morning murk on the M1, the traffic behind obscured by burning engine oil. Destination: Hull, and a workaday overnight passenger ferry bound for Belgium.

The North Sea in February vied with the ship's vibration to prevent sleep, and berthing the following morning was heralded by a resounding thud. This was Zeebrugge, and the opportunity to explore the transport scene, starting with the Kusttram, the tramway that runs for 42 scenic miles along the Belgian coast from Knokke on the Dutch border to De Panne at the French end.

Forty-eight single-ended trams, built in 1982 in France by Le Brugeoise et Nivelles, plied the route. New Bombardier bi-directional trams replaced them in 2023. The Kusttram relies on passengers' honesty when purchasing tickets, but I soon learned that incurring the wrath of ticket inspectors was nothing compared to the perils of missing the *Pride of Bruges* when it set sail for Hull.

Madeira in 2022. A UTIC-bodied Volvo B10M-55 of Horarios de Funchal prepares for a white-knuckle plunge back to the Funchal seafront. P&O Cruises' *Azura* is in the harbour.

The Kusttrams form a small part of the fleet of the Flemish state-owned De Lijn, which has around 400 trams and over 2,000 buses – a diverse fleet that includes VDLs, Volvos, Van Hool integrals and Mercedes-Benz Citaros.

Anyone now visiting Belgium must travel via the Netherlands or France, as the Zeebrugge ferry was withdrawn in March 2021. Fortunately, one job led to another, and the North Sea was great preparation for the notorious Bay of Biscay. Brittany Ferries, running from Portsmouth to Spain, became my employer – and the ferry *Pont-Aven* my home.

After a crossing of 24hr, with only a couple of hours ashore, there was little time to sample the municipal buses of Santander, but long enough to get a flavour of the fleet – older MANs and Citaros, supplemented by new-generation hybrids and electrics. Eventually I obtained employment with P&O Cruises, enabling me to travel farther afield, but I often still crossed the Bay of Biscay where sea sickness pills were *de rigeur*.

Canarian capers

My first cruise ship engagement took me to Gran Canaria, the second largest of the Canary Islands. Until 2000, it was home to three scheduled service fleets – the blue/orange vehicles of Utinsa, the green ones of Salcai, and the bright yellow Guaguas Municipales within the capital, Las Palmas. *Guagua* (pronounced wah-wah) is the vernacular for bus throughout the Canaries.

Salcai and Utinsa, with around 300 vehicles, were combined to form Global in March 2000. The intensive operation in the north, inherited from Utinsa, serves the heavily-populated suburbs of Las Palmas and its rugged hinterland. Tourist services dominate the former Salcai territory of the south.

The main centre of operation is Las Palmas, which has a large and busy bus station at San Telmo. Smaller ones are scattered around the island. The existence of rural can frustrate the sighting of a particular bus if it is so allocated, tucked away in the mountains. Principal depots are in Las Palmas, Campo de Golf (Maspalomas) and Telde, which houses the central works and storage space for new and withdrawn vehicles. The Telde premises can be viewed from above if you are sufficiently athletic, by scaling the surrounding hilly waste ground – with a healthy respect for the prickly cacti. My Spanish is limited to the usual requests for beer and the bill, so I have never requested entry to the site.

Comprehensive services connect all the main towns. The airport is served by route 66 to the southern resorts, the 60 to Las Palmas and the 36 inland to Telde. A few smaller local operators also exist on Gran Canaria, but the overwhelming impression is of a Global monopoly.

It took a decade, but the Global fleet was eventually repainted aquamarine with a large yellow logo. The mainstay of both constituent fleets was the Castrosua CS-40 body on either a Mercedes-Benz or Scania chassis, many of which survived until the mid-2010s. By then, a new generation – Scanias with Castrosua Magnus or Irizar Intercentury bodies – dominated the fleet, but most of these have since been replaced in a fleet renewal programme begun in 2018. Life is tough for these *guaguas*. It might not rain much, but the combination of salty air, heavy loads and tight schedules takes its toll on bodywork and mechanicals. A life

Horario de Funchal`s new Volvo B8RLEs are now very much in charge of the city`s routes. This is one of the short wheelbase version. Bodywork is by Unvi, badged as Camo as a nod to the former owner of the factory. The only older vehicles seen on this day, January 1, 2025, were Volvo B12BLEs like the one in the background.

of around 12 years is swiftly followed by a trip to the island`s metal recyclers.

My passion for buses on Gran Canaria derives not just from the few hours allowed ashore from a cruise ship, but numerous holidays taken over the past 20 years. A day riding the buses will offer great scenery, reasonable fares and a varied fleet. But keeping up to date with the fleet is challenging. The exquisite frustration caused by the absence of information for the enthusiast is maybe part of the mystique of buses abroad.

Putting the fun in Funchal

Normally you only get a few hours in port when a cruise ship docks. How fortunate, then, that a weekly diagram on P&O's *Azura* included a late Monday departure from the mountainous Portuguese island of Madeira, with plenty of time to immerse myself in the city fleet of Horarios de Funchal whose cheerful yellow buses chase each other industriously along the capital`s seafront before fanning out up the steep hillsides to destinations almost up in the clouds.

On my first visit, its fleet included around 60 venerable Volvo B10M-55s bodied by Camo or UTIC; generally ZF automatic, though the earliest ones were manual. They were augmented by various later Volvos, badged as B9Ms and B12Ms. The newest buses were 20 Camo-bodied Volvo B7RLEs dating from 2008.

Like a lark ascending, the old Volvos screeched heavenwards with such alarming progress that heaven indeed seemed a likely destination. But the thrills of an uphill ride were nothing compared to the white-knuckle downhill return to town. Plunging down steep ravines, driver`s leaden foot switching feverishly between accelerator and brake... it was all too much on one occasion even for this salty sea dog. I was soon harrumphing over a poor unsuspecting cactus, which maybe went to glory as the B10Ms now sadly have.

A fleet replacement programme, bringing 129 new buses, was already in progress in 2022; for a limited time, the new rubbed shoulders with the old.

The bus drivers of Funchal are undoubtedly kindly folk who love their families and pets. But once behind the wheel of a B10M a red mist seemed to appear in front of their eyes. Not that it needed it, the impression of a Formula One racing car was further enhanced by what I assume to be locally-crafted replacement differentials which emitted a menacing growl, ascending in pitch with speed.

Even older buses departed Funchal on infrequent country routes to distant outposts, including 40-plus- year-old Volvo B58s, operated by Rodoeste. I resisted these temptations, since missing the ship`s departure would result in dismissal — not to mention the inconvenience of being stranded without a passport.

All are history now. When I returned on New Year`s Day 2025, most of the city fleet had been swept away by new Volvo B8RLEs, some of them bearing the fleet numbers of departed B10Ms. The newcomers — of two lengths — carry Camo Urbis bodies, built by Unvi but badged Camo as a tribute to the former owners of the factory. The B7RLEs of 2008, until recently the newest buses, were now among Funchal's oldest.

Furthermore, in a coup reminiscent of the retirement of Malta`s ancient fleet, all the country buses – some dating back as far as 1979 — were swept away overnight six months earlier by 127 new Ivecos, the original operators' identities were replaced by SIGA, a new transport authority with standardised livery. Nothing lasts forever, does it?

Stranger on the shore

That is what everyone was saying when the last London Routemasters were retired from normal service in 2005, but some of them have defied that maxim.

My purchase of a United States visa brought a significant stretching of my sphere of sailings, allowing me to embark on a Canada/USA odyssey. Following a six-day sea voyage in September 2022, I was greeted by that familiar sight in a lurid pink livery when on the quayside of St John's, Newfoundland.

Gray Line, marketing as Ambassatours, had a significant number of pink RMLs employed on hop-on/hop-off tours for cruise passengers, their livery a nod to the company's support of breast cancer research. They only appear when a cruise ship is in town.

RML2373 was parked alluringly next to the ship, so I hopped on, and was immediately transported back to the best parts of Streatham in the early noughties. Apart from a (Canadian) nearside door and a modest public address system, the interior remained unchanged. The conductress/guide was fiercely proud of her steed, and it seemed churlish to query her claim that the bus dated from 1938; the American cruise passengers were certainly convinced.

Plenty of these Routemaster time warps creaked sedately around St John's and Halifax, Nova Scotia, coaxed along sympathetically by retired bus and lorry drivers. One of their amiable pilots confided in me that spares were occasionally shipped across the pond.

On my last visit in 2024, the Ambassatours fleet had been expanded by the acquisition of red RMs, RMLs and RCLs from the erstwhile Double Deck Tours, Niagara. These had London destination blinds, some even their original AEC engines.

Homeward bound

Many cruise ships to break their journey back to the UK in Lisbon. This welcome diversion affords a stunning scenic cruise along the estuary of the River Tagus, passing the Sanctuary of Christ the King and under a 2km-long suspension bridge reminiscent of San Francisco's Golden Gate.

This was the vision in pink parked next to the cruise ships in St John's, Newfoundland in September 2022. With up to 5,000 potential customers, Gray Line's Routemasters, including RML2373, were kept busy on hop-on/hop-off tours, although breakdowns were not uncommon.

Cruise passengers alight to view the reversing rapids at St John's, caused by the combination of the highest tide range in the world and a fast-flowing river. The Routemasters acquired from Double Deck Tours do not have the addition of a Canadian nearside door, so RCL2255`s emergency door is tied open permanently.

No cable cars climbing halfway to the stars in the Portuguese capital, but the tiny, rickety trams that twist and grind their way over the points and seem to miss walls and parked cars by inches are every bit as exhilarating. Both these and the city`s buses are in a yellow and white that reflects Lisbon`s happy, friendly atmosphere, and are operated by Carris, a publicly-owned body.

For a traditional tram ride, many tourists take the westbound route 28 – a long climb out to Prazeres, passing numerous cobbled squares and historic buildings, aboard a vehicle invariably loaded to the

Pedestrians negotiate a path behind two classic Lisbon trams in August 2024.

Journey's end. A coach turning circle that requires steady nerves and perfect precision, at the cruise terminal at Bridgetown, Barbados.

gunwales. Standing passengers must brace themselves stoically against the constant canting and swaying, and a rudimentary braking system that grinds the tram to an abrupt, jarring halt. The old trams also serve the quieter route 25, leaving the Placa de Figueira in the city centre to follow a different path to the same destination, running parallel to the Tagus.

The trams, numbered 541 to 585, are known as *remodelados* and after several rebuildings and renumberings, they have certain similarities to Trigger's broom. However ,the main bodies certainly date from the early 20th century, and if the period atmosphere is tainted by the Wi-Fi signs on the windows, this is compensated for by some quaint traditions. Drivers occasionally climb out to poke a pole into a hole in the road to change the points; the destination boxes, which sit proud of the roof, are changed by pointing a mirror on a stick out of the window.

The tram men's concentration is stretched to the limit by disrespectful road users, congestion, parked cars, confused tourists and jaywalking pedestrians. No wonder

you often see them puffing with euphoric relief on a cigarette at the terminus.

The tram routes seem straightforward, but Lisbon's bus network is vast and complex. I spent considerable time staring in confusion at the complicated maps at bus stops. Eventually I pinpointed route 736 to Odivelas as a way of seeing the real Lisbon, away from the tourist trail, travelling north from the centre out into the suburbs. Persona non grata in London, the Citaro bendybus seemed perfectly at home on the 736, pressing urgently onwards with a constant ebb and flow of passengers.

Lisbon is steeped in culture, a truly global city and the westernmost one in Europe. It is often the last port of call on a cruise ship itinerary, and the last one of this whistle-stop tour. You can always rely on a humble musician to find ways of saving money, and my advice for visitors to a European city is to avoid expensive organised coach excursions and buy a travelcard, which, for just a few Euros, will enable a couple of hours' sightseeing on local buses.

Just get back before the ship sails... ∎

The availability of four rear-entrance, front-exit Burlingham-bodied AEC Regal IVs, no longer required by Rochdale, enabled Albert Burrows to start balancing the demand and supply of road staff in Lancaster. The rear entrance was removed and seating upped to 44. At Damside Street bus station in May 1965, 715 (JDK 711) was continuing to perform good service. The lower destination blind left passengers in no doubt as to whom they should tender their fare. An East Lancs-bodied Leyland Titan PD2/41 is in the background, as are four Ribble Leylands. IAIN MacGREGOR

A man of influence

As he progressed rapidly as a municipal general manager in the 1960s, Albert Burrows introduced one-person-operated buses with East Lancs bodies and dual doors to four fleets. **ANDREW BABBS** tells his story and that of the buses he was responsible for ordering.

In his short life — he died aged 53 — Albert Burrows was general manager of four municipal undertakings and director general of a PTE, all of which purchased dual-door buses with East Lancs bodywork, one-person operated using Ultimate ticket machines. They were his legacy.

He was born in Warrington on November 3, 1919, second son of tram driver John Burrows and his wife Ada. After grammar school, he became a clerk with Warrington Corporation's passenger transport department and returned there after war service with the Royal Engineers. Career progression took him to larger municipal undertakings, as a commercial assistant in Nottingham and commercial officer at Portsmouth.

His first appointment as a general manager was in 1956 in his native Lancashire, as GM and engineer at the Lancaster City Transport Department, which operated 31 double-deckers and 14 single-deckers; all were crew operated, all but two with rear entrances. It continued along similar lines, ordering another nine Leyland Titan PD2s with East Lancs bodies, with two delivered in 1957 and two in 1958.

The forward-entrance pair were halfcab AEC Regal IIIs which Burrows adapted for one-person operation, complementing them with a rear-entrance 1952 Daimler CVG6 single-decker rebuilt to a similar layout and a quartet of four-year-old underfloor-engined AEC Regal IVs with Burlingham 44-seat bodies purchased from Rochdale. The Regal IVs' rear exit doors were removed before arrival

Albert Burrows.

at Lancaster, but they retained a roof level destination blind box adjacent to where they had been.

One-person operation helped reduce the staffing requirement – Ribble also was short of conductors in Lancaster – but a network review had more impact. Burrows saved eight vehicles by rejigging Lancaster's routes to operate via the bus station and linked them together in groups, each operated either by crew double-deckers or driver-only single-deckers. One bus served three or four outer termini in sequence, always running via the bus station. Each leg had a different route number and ran in one direction only.

New ticket machines – five-roll Bell Punch Ultimates – were introduced across the network. They were fast to operate and provided more information about the number of tickets of each value sold.

In a move repeated later in his career, Burrows changed the five outstanding Titans to single-deck Leyland Tiger Cubs, retaining the body order at East Lancs. These arrived in 1958 and 1959 and were the first Tiger Cubs into service in the country with Pneumo-cyclic semi-automatic transmission. They provided driver-only capability across the single-deck fleet.

Stop dwell time was longer than for conductor-operated services, but this could be reduced with dual-door single-deckers which allowed people off while others got on. Convinced of the benefits, in March 1961 he ordered three Leyland Leopard L1s with East Lancs dual-door bodywork but moved on to his next general managership before they arrived.

While at Lancaster, he was awarded a Road Transport Research Fellowship by the Institute of Transport. His subject was 'Industrial relations in the transport industry in Great Britain and Europe' for which he visited many undertakings and gained insights into relationships between trade unions and management. The results proved useful ten years later.

Albert Burrows's legacy for Barrow was six dual-door East Lancs-bodied Leyland Leopard L1s delivered in 1963. Its previous single-deckers were a Massey-bodied Royal Tiger and Tiger Cub. East Lancs matched that body design as closely as possible, hence the squat looks and flat windscreens. This view shows 68 (JEO 768) surrounded by Park Royal-bodied Titan PD2s in Hindpool Road garage. ANDREW BABBS COLLECTION

Twenty 36ft rear-engined single-deckers with dual-door Neepsend bodies to East Lancs design were supplied to Chesterfield in 1967/68. The Panthers, with front radiator grille, included 83 (SRB 83F), still running in 1983. ANDREW BABBS COLLECTION

Burrows goes to Barrow

Burrows became GM and engineer at Barrow-in-Furness from April 1, 1961, succeeding Thomas Lord on his appointment to Leeds City Transport. The 63-vehicle Barrow undertaking was the municipal farthest away in Lancashire from where he was born and began his career. He was one of five interviewed for the vacancy and his move from Lancaster was announced the week before Christmas in 1960.

The all-Leyland fleet comprised 60 open platform rear entrance Titan PD2 double-deckers, three Leyland Royal Tiger and one Tiger Cub single-deckers. Fifty of the PD2s had come in a postwar renewal between 1949 and 1951, the other ten in 1958. The Royal Tigers dated from 1952 and 1955, the Tiger Cub from 1959.

Ten more PD2s were on order with Massey bodies. Burrows may have been consulted about their specification, for a change was made from vacuum braked, exposed radiator PD2/40s to air braked PD2A/27s with the St Helens-style glassfibre engine cover. The Massey bodies had a forward entrance, a new feature for Barrow. They entered service around six months after his arrival, by which time he was planning to introduce driver-only operation.

He secured council authority to order six Leyland Leopard L1s, with 42-seat East Lancs dual-door bodies. The specification was almost an exact copy of the three he had bequeathed to Lancaster. The style of the East Lancs bodies, however, mimicked the Royal Tigers with a shallow roof and deeply raked driver's windscreen.

History repeated itself in another way, as Burrows spent less than two years in Barrow and moved on before those Leopard arrived. He had now ordered nine dual-door buses and, as yet, possessed no operating experience of them. His next appointment changed that.

A dalliance in Derbyshire

He moved to Derbyshire as general manager in Chesterfield, succeeding Edward Deakin who had become GM in Bradford. When he arrived in January 1963, he inherited orders for ten dual-door single-deckers — two Leyland Leopard L1s and eight AEC Reliances, all with Park Royal bodies to a BET design — and 18 Daimler front-engined double-deckers with forward entrances.

A further 12 Reliances were ordered before any of these arrived, this time with 42-seat two-door bodies to be supplied by East Lancs. With the first ten buses due in early 1964, agreement was reached with the Transport & General Workers Union for their introduction. Drivers of one-person operated buses received a 15% wage increase and other drivers and conductors were assured there would be no redundancies. At the end of 1964, Chesterfield was still 50 short of its requirement for 500 road staff.

As in Lancaster, driver-only operation was accelerated by purchasing three secondhand single-deckers. These were London Transport's experimental dual-door RW-class

Reliances with Willowbrook bodies. Their Monocontrol semi-automatic gearboxes offered an alternative to the manual gearboxes on the ten new buses.

The order for 12 Reliances placed in 1963 was followed by another for ten the following year; all arrived in 1965. Their bodies, constructed by East Lancs's associate Neepsend Coachworks in Sheffield, had non-opening panoramic windows and forced air ventilation from vents above the windscreen, with the fresh air delivered through ducts within the overhead luggage racks.

Next on Burrows's agenda was the replacement of double-deckers on busier routes. Chesterfield borrowed a new dual-door Leyland Panther from Kingston upon Hull for two weeks in May 1965, trialling it on a different route each day. Hull 175 performed well with its wide doorways receiving passenger approbation. Orders were placed in mid-June for ten each of the Panther and Daimler Roadliner with dual-door East Lancs bodies. These also arrived after he moved on to his next appointment.

Into the big league

That appointment, announced in February 1966, was a surprise to many. At 46, Burrows was leaving Chesterfield,

with its 130 vehicles, to head Liverpool Corporation Passenger Transport with just over 1,100, succeeding William Hall who retired after 18 years in post. This was a plum position, managing Britain's fourth largest municipal fleet.

He rapidly assessed the undertaking and its future direction, building on his experience in Lancaster and Chesterfield, announcing in October 1966 that an order for 130 MCW-bodied Leyland Atlanteans was truncated to 60, with the remaining 70 substituted by Panthers with 47-seat dual-door MCW bodies suitable for one-person operation.

He also received approval to seek tenders for 65 more dual-door single-deckers which were ordered in summer 1967 — another 40 MCW-bodied Panthers and 25 Bristol RELL6Gs with 45-seat Park Royal bodywork, the only REs that Park Royal ever bodied. Those 135 single-deckers gave Liverpool the largest fleet of them then in any large city outside London.

None of the Panthers arrived in 1967, but in preparation for their introduction the fare structure was coarsened to make the drivers' task easier and have fares which would readily translate into decimal currency in February 1971.

A pay increase of £1 3s (£1.15) was agreed for drivers and conductors, subject to the approval of the

Liverpool's rear-engined single-deckers included 25 Bristol RELL6Gs with Park Royal bodywork to the corporation's specification. This shows 2020 (SKB 690G) at Mann Island in Merseyside PTE livery.

A May 1977 picture of L871 (FKF 871E), one of the 50 MCW-bodied Atlanteans that Liverpool had converted to dual-door layout by Pennine Coachcraft in 1968.

government's Prices & Incomes Board (PIB). Impatient with the delay in granting approval, crews went on unofficial strike for 11 weeks until the PIB agreed to the increase. The first Panthers arrived during the strike and entered service from July 1, 1968.

The undertaking's 1968 annual report bemoaned "appalling delays by the bodybuilder"; MCW was fulfilling orders then from London Transport for 650 AEC Merlins. Leyland suggested supplying 20 AEC Swifts instead of Panthers to expedite delivery.

Almost lost among the trade press reports of the strike and the Panthers entering service was a return to favouring double-deckers, agreement having been reached with road staff to operate them without conductors. Following the conversion at Edge Lane works of a three-year-old Atlantean to dual-door layout with its staircase moved to the centre and seating capacity reduced from 76 to 71, the corporation contracted Seddon's Pennine Coachcraft business in Oldham to undertake similar conversions of the 50 newest Atlanteans and modify the next newest 50 for driver-only operation while retaining their single-door layout.

He secured committee approval in 1968 for 65 new double-deckers, 33ft (10m) long to maintain a high seating capacity in dual-door layout. As with the single-deckers a year earlier, 40 would come from Leyland (Atlantean PDR2/1) and 25 from Bristol (VRT/LH6G), the latter being the first municipal order for double-deckers since Bristol

was able to trade again on the open market in 1965 and unusual in having the optional higher chassis frame.

The body orders marked a break from MCW, Alexander 79-seaters on the Atlanteans (a bespoke design for Liverpool, the L-type) and East Lancs 80-seaters on the Bristols. A repeat order placed in 1969, shortly before the undertaking passed to the new Merseyside PTE, was for another 120 of the same — 85 Alexander-bodied Atlanteans and 35 East Lancs-bodied Bristols. Barely half a dozen of the Atlanteans and none of the Bristols were delivered before the PTE took over in December 1969.

Same place, big new job

Merseyside's was one of the first four PTEs created under the Transport Act 1968, each the executive arm of the passenger transport authorities (PTA) in the largest English city regions outside London. They were headed by a director general, with a wider role than a municipal general manager, responsible for developing and delivering coordinated surface public transport.

Albert Burrows was shortlisted for all four. Three — the first to announce their appointments — selected candidates with other backgrounds, with West Midlands the only one to appoint a bus manager, London Transport's chief commercial and planning officer, Frederick Lloyd. Selnec, covering Greater Manchester, chose a council chief executive, Tony Harrison who headed the Bolton authority. Tyneside, with the construction of the Metro light railway a high priority,

The last 60 Atlantean PDR2/1s ordered by Liverpool had an 80-seat version of Alexander's L-type body with the exit door directly behind the front wheels. This June 1978 photograph shows 1223 (XKC 850K), new to Merseyside PTE in December 1971, a year before Albert Burrows's sudden death.

selected Tony Ridley, a civil engineer with the Greater London Council.

Burrows was spared the ignominy of Merseyside going the same way. His appointment was announced on July 14, 1969, less than four months before the PTE took over the Mersey ferries and corporation buses in Liverpool, Birkenhead and Wallasey, keeping the Liverpool fleet green and cream, while combining elements of the other two into a blue and cream Wirral livery.

Beside day-to-day running of an expanded bus undertaking, there were operating agreements to negotiate with the National Bus Company and British Rail and plans to implement for new rail tunnels under Liverpool.

As for the buses, the 125 Atlanteans arrived on schedule, but the Bristols were delayed by a fire at the East Lancs factory in which one was destroyed, reducing the first intake to 24 placed in service between August 1970 and January 1971 with H and J suffix registrations; there was no bus 2050. The 35 numbered from 2051 upwards arrived later in 1971. The Bristols were garaged at Garston and Walton, respectively in the south and north of Liverpool.

There ended the Burrows legacy of dual-door East Lancs-bodied buses on which drivers issued tickets from Ultimate machines, 51 single-deckers and 59 double-deckers for four undertakings between 1961 and 1971.

Fifty dual-door MCW-bodied 33ft Daimler Fleetlines ordered for the Wirral were changed to 9.4m with a single door. Dual-door 33ft double-deckers fell from favour nationally, shorter dwell times at busy stops outweighed by their less favourable power-to-weight ratio, higher operating cost and the greater risk of passengers being injured, sometimes fatally, when exiting by a door that was difficult for drivers to see. The second door on the last 60 of Merseyside's PDR2s was farther forward, directly behind the front wheels.

The 9.5m Atlantean AN68 with 75-seat single-door body became the PTE's standard double-decker. An initial order called for 200 with Alexander's new AL body and 50 from East Lancs, supplemented by 60 similar Alexander bodies on Atlantean PDR1A/1 Special chassis from a cancelled Midland Red order. The connection with East Lancs remained.

Such was Albert Burrows's reputation that he became The Omnibus Society's president in 1971 and was elected president of the Association of Public Passenger Transport Operators (APPTO) for 1972/73, a post he held for three months before his sudden death on December 23, 1972, a Saturday. Over 500 attended his funeral, many representing sectors across the industry.

His successor as director general was a former colleague, FA Moffat, who had spent most of his career with Liverpool Corporation and the PTE to which he returned after three years as director of operations at West Midlands PTE. The APPTO presidency was filled by Edward Deakin, his predecessor at Chesterfield a decade before. ■

South Yorkshire PTE was the first British operator to identify the potential for articulated buses as an alternative to double-deckers on routes where its cheap fares were generating large numbers of short distance passengers. It tested this left-hand-drive Leyland demonstrator in July 1977 with chassis and body by Leyland's Danish subsidiary, DAB, and coupling system by Swiss manufacturer Saurer. This was a 'puller' artic, with a horizontal underfloor engine in the front section. It was photographed turning into Pond Street bus station in Sheffield, with the Park Hill estate in the background. TONY WILSON

Bendybuses in the British Isles

Used widely around the world, articulated single-deckers — bendybuses — have played a limited and sometimes controversial role as mass people movers in Britain and Ireland over the past half century

South Yorkshire took delivery of ten 'puller' artics in 1978/79 for its free Cityliner service in Sheffield, for which they were painted in this special livery, but a pay dispute led to their early withdrawal. Five were 63-seat MAN SG192s built in Germany, of which 2005 (CLM 346T) was the first to be registered. MAN coined the name Bendibus for them. By April 1982, the quintet had been leased to City of Oxford, and they moved later within the National Bus Company to Midland Red North. TONY WILSON

South Yorkshire's other five were Leyland-DABs with 60-seat Leyland National bodies built at Workington, of which 2008 (FHE 291V) was one of two leased subsequently to McGill's Bus Service of Barrhead for a new service into Glasgow city centre. Their green and orange stripes were changed to McGill's red and grey. IAIN MacGREGOR

South Yorkshire reintroduced bendybuses in 1985 when it purchased 13 Leyland-DABs with Danish-built bodywork. Still in service in Sheffield in May 1999, by which time First had acquired Mainline, the PTE's former bus operation, was 2004 (C104 HDT), operating a shuttle service to Meadowhall shopping complex. TONY WILSON

Transport for London embraced the operation of bendybuses on a big scale, with 430 low-floor 49-seat Mercedes-Benz Citaro 'pusher' artics, with engine in the rear section, introduced between 2002 and 2008 to help handle a big growth in passenger numbers. Some replaced Routemasters. Boris Johnson, elected Mayor of London in May 2008, ordered their removal and the last were withdrawn in December 2011. Those operated by Stagecoach included 23037 (LX04 KZJ), photographed in Manor Park. MARK LYONS

Travel West Midlands bought 11 of Scania's articulated OmniCity, including 6023 (BX54 DND) branded for Birmingham service 67. MARK LYONS

First was an early adopter of bendybuses and in 2005 commissioned Wrightbus to develop its tram-like StreetCar body on a modified Volvo B7LA chassis for FTR (text shorthand for 'future'), a concept for bus-based rapid transit services that could be introduced more quickly and at less cost than light rail schemes. Forty were built for routes in York, Leeds and Swansea, but the last were withdrawn in 2016. This was First York 19010 (YK06 AUA). MARK LYONS

Translink's cross-city Glider service in Belfast, introduced in 2018 with the first of 34 Belgian-built Van Hool Exqui.City hybrid bendybuses, is the most extensive bus rapid transit service in the UK. The Liverpool City Region mayor wants to replicate the concept in Merseyside, but Van Hool no longer manufactures buses, just coaches. MARK LYONS

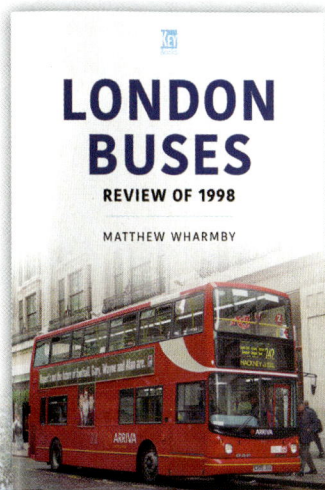

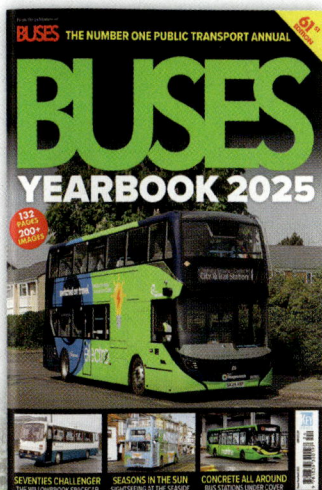

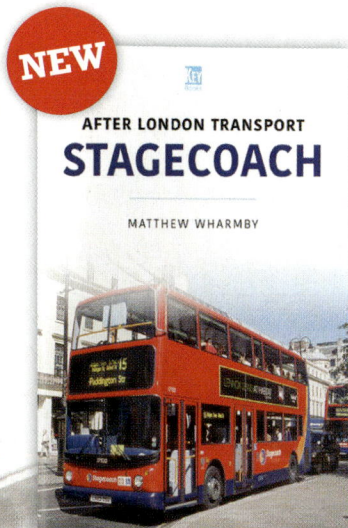

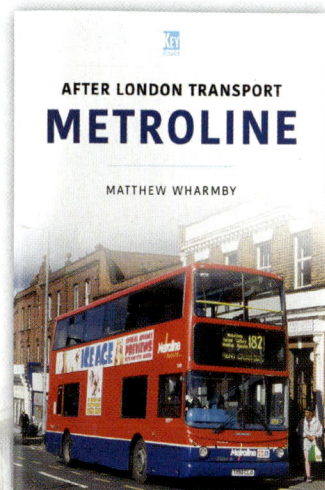

The most numerous type then in the Merseybus fleet was the Alexander AL-bodied Leyland Atlantean. Typifying these is 1890 (XEM 890W), an AN68C/1R new in 1981, heading along Lord Street, Liverpool in April 1988. Merseybus experimented with different liveries before settling on maroon and cream; a few vehicles carried this two-tone green scheme.

Deregulated on Merseyside

JOHN ROBINSON gives a flavour of the bus scene in Liverpool city region during the first ten years following the upheaval of deregulation on October 26, 1986

Fareway Passenger Services, based in Kirkby, was Merseyside's first major newcomer to bus operation post-deregulation and also the largest. It began operations in February 1987 with a striking blue and yellow livery. The impact of Fareway is apparent from this view in Kirkby bus station in March 1988 with a solitary Merseybus Leyland Atlantean AN68/Alexander AL-type, 1878 (XEM 878W), outnumbered by four Fareway vehicles. Nearest the camera is former Greater Manchester Transport standard-type Daimler Fleetline/Northern Counties YNA 352M while former Merseyside PTE GKA 78N, an East Lancs-bodied Bristol VRT/SL2/6G, is behind. Fareway introduced fleetnumbers later that year. MTL acquired Fareway in 1993.

Although the bulk of Merseyside's bus operations remained in the hands of the successors to Merseyside Passenger Transport Executive (MPTE) and the National Bus Company (NBC) between 1986 and 1996, an eclectic mix of other operators filled the vacuum from those organisations reducing fleet size and staffing levels.

Whereas near-neighbour Manchester experienced the growth of many new, but relatively small operators, Liverpool witnessed the opposite with a smaller number of larger newcomers. The three best-known — Fareway, Liverbus and Liver Line — were set up by former PTE employees; these fledgling operators then began to compete with Merseybus, the PTE's arm's length company — full name Merseyside Transport Ltd, later abbreviated to MTL.

At the same time, some established coach operators, including Liverpool-based Amberline and Toppings, and Wigan-based Shearings, moved into bus operations for the first time.

A third dynamic was out-of-town operators entering Merseyside. These included PMT, which set up an operation in Wirral called Red Rider, which later expanded significantly when it acquired Crosville's Birkenhead and Chester depots in the final breaking up of Crosville in 1990.

Wirral experienced an additional incursion from north Wales operator Blythin, St Asaph, trading as Gold Star,

which set up a Birkenhead in 1988 called Busman Buses and introduced new services using Daimler Fleetlines delivered new to the town's Laird Street depot and disposed of by the PTE as it downsized at deregulation.

Other interlopers were GM Buses North and GM Buses South, successors to Greater Manchester PTE when its bus operations were split. In retaliation for MTL setting up its predatory MTL Manchester operation, GM Buses North established itself in north Liverpool while GM Buses South focused on Wirral from May 1994 with Birkenhead & District, which revived the former Birkenhead Corporation livery of blue and cream; it lasted just over a year, ceasing operations in July 1995.

Forty years on from deregulation, the Liverpool City Region, in common with the other former PTE areas in England, plans to bring bus services back into public control from 2026 by adopting the franchising model first used by Greater Manchester with its Bee Network, which became fully-operational in January 2025.

In preparation for this, Arriva and Stagecoach buses have begun to appear in a uniform Metro livery which, like the Bee Network's, is yellow although with the addition of grey and black. It bears more than a passing resemblance to the livery used by Merseytravel, as the PTE renamed itself, on some buses on tendered services in the early 1990s, yellow also being the base colour of the Merseyrail electric train network. ■

Ribble's territory was reduced significantly during 1986 with the Carlisle and Penrith operations passing to Cumberland and those in Merseyside and Wigan to the new North Western company. Newly delivered to that fleet in March 1988 were ten Dodge S56s with Northern Counties bodywork, including 95 (E95 WCM) operating a service from Kirkby to Aintree. Destination blinds had yet to be fitted.

Merseyside PTE purchased 15 Alexander RV-bodied Volvo Ailsa B55s, two in 1982 and the remainder in 1984. All were allocated to Laird Street, Birkenhead depot. The driver is climbing into the cab of the first of the 1984 batch, 0069 (A151 HLV), at the Virginia Road terminus in New Brighton in May 1988. Merseybus branding has been applied to the PTE's Verona green and cream livery.

PMT, sold by NBC to its management in December 1986, set up its Red Rider operation in Moreton, Wirral. ECW-bodied Bristol RELL6L 217 (PVT 217L), new in 1972, stands at Seacombe Ferry bus station in May 1988, operating to nearby Liscard Village. Within two years PMT's presence on Merseyside expanded considerably when it purchased the Crosville depot at Rock Ferry, Birkenhead from Drawlane Transport, along with the depot in Chester as part of the final dismantling of Crosville which also transferred Northwich to North Western.

Speke-based Arena Coaches came on the scene in 1989 when it tendered successfully for some supported services. Former West Midlands PTE NOC 489R, a 1977 Leyland Fleetline with MCW body, was in Prescot bus station in May 1990, operating evening and Sunday service 247 (Prescot-Huyton). This vehicle ran subsequently with two other Merseyside operators City Fleet of Bootle and Village of Garston.

Warrington coach operator Barry Cooper became part of the Mayne group in 1982 and operated bus services in the town and farther afield following deregulation. East Lancs-bodied Leyland Leopard PSU4/2R EHB 259G, new to Merthyr Tydfil Corporation in 1968 and latterly with Stonier, Goldenhill, was also in Prescot bus station in May 1990. It was carrying a handwritten paper bill in the windscreen for servcce 52 (Warrington-Prescot), formerly Crosville's H2 (Warrington-Liverpool) which was cut back to Prescot.

Following deregulation, Wigan-based Shearings expanded beyond its core market of coach holidays to operate bus services in various parts of England. It became a major operator of them in Merseyside, Greater Manchester and Cheshire with new and secondhand vehicles. Leyland Tiger 62 (G62 RND), new in 1989 and photographed in Baldwin Street, St Helens in June 1991, was one of 40 with Alexander (Belfast) N-type bodywork in the fleet. Overtaking is Halton Leyland National 23 (BTB 23T). Shearings' bus services passed to Timeline, a management buyout, in 1992, retaining the Shearings livery, and were taken over later by First Manchester.

Hatton of St Helens is the only operator in this feature still running bus services in Merseyside in 2025 under the same name. YCW 847N, an East Lancs-bodied Bristol RESL6G new to Burnley & Pendle in 1974, was in Westfield Street, St Helens in June 1991.

Liver Line, established in 1988, was another new start operator that challenged Merseybus in Liverpool. Its double-deckers included 46 (PHG 775P), an East Lancs-bodied Leyland Atlantean new to Hyndburn in 1976, photographed in Hood Street Gyratory, Liverpool in June 1991 on service 38 from Central Bus Station to Halewood. Merseybus 1911 (XEM 911W), an Alexander-bodied Atlantean five years younger, is passing on service 87 from Pier Head to Woodend Avenue (Speke Garage). North Western acquired Liver Line in autumn 1993.

MTL expanded into Greater Manchester in 1993 with its MTL Manchester operation. One of the last vehicles still in that operation's original livery in May 1994, heading along Oldham Road, Failsworth, was East Lancs-bodied Leyland Atlantean AN68A/1R 1740 (LKF 740R), new to Merseyside PTE in 1977. It was operating service 82 (Waterhead-Manchester).

Nowadays, Irizar exports substantial numbers of its Spanish-made integral vehicles and bodies on Scania chassis to the UK. Its first attempt to crack this market was in the early 1980s with the unusual step-window Urko of which a mere 14 reached these shores. In Wellington Street coach station in Leeds was Volvo B58 HPL 322V, operated by Maddren Travel of Billingham, initially a regular operator of duplicate coaches before undertaking contracts in its own right. RICHARD SIMONS

National coaching variety

The white livery was near universal across England and Wales, but **HOWARD BERRY** provides a reminder of some of the non-standard coaches operated on the National Express network in the 1980s and early 1990s

In the 1970s and early 1980s it would have been a chassis from the Leyland empire with Plaxton, Duple or (shudder) Willowbrook bodywork; then in the late 1980s and early 1990s it was the Volvo B10M Plaxton Expressliner, and nowadays it's the Caetano Levante.

Yes, I'm talking about the 'standard' National Express coach. A combination of a lack of viable alternatives — and before those of you of a certain age start shouting 'but what about the Bedford YMT and Ford R-series?', they really didn't make much of an inroad into National Bus Company fleets — plus an attempt to get a reasonably standardised operational fleet makes it appear there hasn't been much vehicular variety on the UK's white coach network over the past 50-plus years. Or has there?

Two years before the deregulation of Britain's bus services was on the government's agenda, the National Bus Company (NBC) began to break its southern regional subsidiaries into smaller businesses. They also began to enjoy what appeared to be a loosening of the corporate buying shackles and broadened their horizons when sourcing vehicles, even more so when they were privatised.

Add to this the relaxation of National Express's contract process, now permitting independent and municipal operators to undertake diagrams in their own right, rather than just operating duplication runs, and you had a veritable feast of interesting vehicles out and about on the network.

As an example, when I started working for the newly privatised Western National in 1987, the coach fleet was predominantly a Leyland/Plaxton combination. One year later, it contained three Neoplan Skyliners, three Duple 425s, two Van Hool Astrons and several DAF MBs.

Stick a private plate on something exotic looking and no one will know how old it really is. Neoplan Jetliner 553 KRO was new in 1982 as EFW 854X and was the second single-deck Neoplan delivered to a UK operator. This shows it in the employ of Rotherham Travel Services, a short-lived operation formed to take over SUT's coaching operations in 1989. RICHARD SIMONS

East Kent had a penchant for the AEC Reliance and liked to undertake the odd cheeky rebuild. None came odder than the batch of ten 1973 Duple Dominant-bodied Reliances to receive new Berkhof Esprit bodies in 1983/84. Their original bodies were removed by the Ensign dealership, which also carried out sufficient modifications to the chassis to justify them receiving age-related registrations, as seen on 8203 (A203 TAR), originally HFN 59L, in Brighton in 1991. RICHARD SIMONS

We couldn't believe it, these new-fangled space age (mainly) foreign things coming down into deepest darkest Cornwall...Thomas Tilling must have been turning in his grave.

Some NBC fleets broke away from the norm several years before privatisation, National London and United Auto with their Bovas, for example, and National Travel East had some exotic Jonckheere-bodied Volvo B10Ms delivered in 1984. Plus, there were those magnificent looking but spectacularly unreliable Duple Goldliner-bodied Dennis Falcon Vs, the almost as unreliable but majestic MCW Metroliner, and several growling Gardner-engined Plaxton Paramount 4000s.

What follow here are some of the more diverse vehicles that were on the network during that period from the 1980s to the 1990s — an era that I look back at with great fondness, with happy memories, but quite possibly through rose tinted glasses. ■

Only 23 Leyland Tigers were bodied by Jonckheere, and West Yorkshire PTE purchased three Jubilee P50-bodied examples to join its Metrocoach operation. Originally registered B611 VWU, 1611 (GSU 340) was reaching journey's end in Leeds. RICHARD SIMONS

While Caetano is National Express's current preferred bodybuilder, its products were few and far between on the network. Only seven Caetano Algarve-bodied Leyland Tigers were built, and five of them were delivered in white — two for National Express's own small in-house fleet and three for Smiths Shearings. One of the latter was C358 FVU seen swinging out of Bury Interchange in 1987. ALAN SNATT

Wessex of Bristol was one of the largest operators on the National Express network. Having stepped in at short notice when incumbent operators withdrew from their contracts, it had outstations in Birmingham and Walton on the Naze. Wessex was the only company to operate the MCW Metro Hi-Liner on regular National Express work, having two of the 21 built. Departing Doncaster South Bus Station on service 730 back home to Bristol was 131 (C131 CFB). RICHARD SIMONS

A real rarity now, in the shape of D310 TWB, a DAF SB2300 with the last of only ten Van Rooijen Odyssee bodies imported into the UK between 1984 and 1987 (seven on DAFs and three on Volvo B10M-62s. It was probably the most photographed of the ten thanks to it getting about a bit on the National Express network when operated by Bennett's of Warrington and was the regular performer on the Warrington-Edinburgh run on which it was photographed leaving Buchanan bus station in Glasgow. It was new to KM of Lundwood as D417 SKU. DARREN BENNETT

You don't have to be exotic to be a rarity and I'm going to stick my neck out here and say that while several National Express operators ran the Duple 340, only Bebb of Llantwit Fardre, Dorset Travel Services and Limebourne of London operated the lowheight version, the Duple 320. One of the latter's was Leyland Tiger D133 HML, passing through Barnsley on the 564 to Halifax. ALAN SNATT

With coaches built by Kässbohrer Setra being at the top end of the price range, it's no surprise they were not the first choice for operators undertaking National Express contracts. Only Bebb of Llantwit Fardre and Chenery's of Dickleburgh used them in any significant numbers, Chenery's purchasing several examples from Bebb's including D704 NUH, photographed on layover in London Victoria Coach Station before heading back to Norwich. ALAN SNATT

United Counties, by then owned by Stagecoach, made a surprise purchase in 1989 of FAP Sanos S315-21 100 (G100 JNV), a Yugoslavian-built cut-price version of the Mercedes-Benz O303. It was one of 29 imported by Ensign and marketed as the Ensign Charisma. It was leaving London Victoria for Rugby when still relatively new. ALAN SNATT

Funny how your memory plays tricks on you as I was sure Dorset Travel Services had a fleet of Berkhof Excellence-bodied MAN 16.290s when, in fact, it had the only two imported into the UK. L331/2 BFX were new to DTS in 1993, with the former waiting time in Leicester's St Margaret's bus station. RICHARD SIMONS

Shepperton subterfuge

PAUL ROBERTS had a starring role in a 1984 advertising campaign by National Holidays

I had the privilege of being the driver in a 30sec television commercial advert made for National Holidays in December 1983 and broadcast after Christmas as people made their holiday plans.

The main action was filmed at Shepperton Film Studios, but a preliminary scene was produced at Midland Red's central works in Birmingham with a close-up of a signwriter finishing off a large blue letter 'S' before the camera changed to a wide shot revealing the name National Holidays. The signwriter gave the all-clear and the coach drove off to its holiday destination. The lettering was made of coloured adhesive decals, but the public was not to know that.

It used eight-month-old Leyland Tiger 561 (YGY 640Y), one of three recently transferred to Midland Red (Express) from National Travel (London). Its Plaxton Paramount 3500 body had National Holidays lettering on the nearside only, ready for filming.

With A-prefix registrations already being issued, the powers that be decided that this coach needed one, too. Once within the private roads at Shepperton, it assumed the identity of Tiger 556 (A656 VDA), which was somewhere on the M1 between Birmingham and London and was in National Express Rapide livery. It had a central emergency door, unlike YGY 640Y which had the emergency door at the rear.

Most Midland Red coaches had semi-automatic gearboxes, but the London trio had manual ones and this one's clutch had been replaced and needed to bed in. That was far from ideal for filming an unladen vehicle which behaved more like a vertical take-off aeroplane than a vehicle gliding away gently.

The director ordered several changes as take after take continued. One involved hanging black cloths from poles to look like hills and peaks reflecting in the side of the coach. A few Equity card-registered actors were to play the part of passengers, sat inside by the windows but it was soon decided that it had to be all or nothing. He decided it looked better without them.

He then decreed that 'rubbish' inside the windscreen — the sun visor and its guide rails — spoilt the shot. Our Midland Red mechanic produced a screw driver and removed them in a couple of minutes. Every couple of takes, a studio technician produced a bucket of whitewash to cover my tyre tracks and return the floor to pristine condition.

After 18 or 19 takes — I lost count — the director picked up his megaphone to announce, "It's a wrap", whereupon the studio erupted into cheering and applause. Filming was over.

My 30sec of fame was shown regularly on ITV that winter but my VHS copy has long since disappeared. Did anyone ever spot that National coach running legally on false plates and does anybody still have a copy of the film? ∎

Grilles and spills

STUART EMMETT describes the twin-grilled Cave-Browne-Cave heating and ventilation system, a clever idea let down by its propensity to emit boiling water. Most of the pictures are from his own collection.

The Cave-Browne-Cave (CBC) heating and ventilation system, distinguished by large upper-deck grilles, was a defining feature of the Guy Wulfrunian and many Bristol double-deckers in the 1950s and 1960s, and of examples of a few other types.

It was developed in the late 1940s and followed an approach from the Ministry of Transport to the Society of Motor Manufacturers & Traders (SMMT) about "unhygienic and unpleasant conditions" on buses. This query was passed to the Motor Industry Research Association (MIRA) and taken up by its technical director, Wing Commander Thomas Reginald Cave-Browne-Cave (1886-1969), who was also professor of engineering at Southampton University.

He designed a system that reduced the power loss from the engine radiator fan, improved heating and ventilation for the passengers, kept costs low by being easily adaptable to existing buses and minimised the use of moving parts. It converted all the engine heat to become internal air conditioning, with the aim that it would also eliminate condensation.

Its radiator(s) gave good air flow, and with double-deckers, the CBC system eventually had two small engine radiators placed above the driver's cab roof level at the front outer corners of body. For single-deckers, eventually there was one long radiator in the front panel below the windscreen.

Key parts were the wax capsule-operated Variance shutters that keep the coolant at optimum temperature; the aim being for the engine coolant water to be pumped around the radiators.

In cold weather, air passing through these radiators was diverted internally by flaps, and on double-deckers the left radiator went into the upper saloon and the right one to the lower deck. In hot weather, the flaps could be changed by using push-pull levers in the driver's cab roof to divert all the hot air to the outside of the vehicle.

The conventional front radiator grille was not required, as the movement of the vehicle was usually adequate to cool the engine without the need for a fan or radiator in front of the engine, but it was usually retained to maintain air flow over the engine.

Southampton City Transport became involved in 1949 and converted new Guy Arab III FTR 509 that became the testbed for the system. After experiments by Prof Cave-Browne-Cave, a final design was produced which operated satisfactorily for six years and needed little maintenance. An unexpected bonus was that the bus

The final radiator and repositioned air intake/radiator on experimental Southampton Guy Arab III 162 (FTR509).

Lincolnshire Road Car 757 (GBE 844), a 1950 Bristol K5G with highbridge ECW body, GBE844 was rebuilt in 1958 after an accident and fitted with this style of front intakes and a Lodekka cowl.

West Yorkshire Road Car SGL7 (JWU 877), a Bristol LL5G fitted with a CBC system in 1953. The air intake was on the top of the destination indicator, with an out-take vent behind

remained cleaner inside, as the constant flow of air carried the dust outside through the open platform.

Southampton installed the CBC system between March 1956 and 1959 to the last two batches of its Park Royal-bodied Arabs, HTR 51-60 new in 1952 and LOW 210-20 from 1953.

Tilling takes it up

With the original Southampton installation reported to give a "pleasant experience", the state-owned Tilling Group was approached and authorised a modification to a 1940 Hants & Dorset Bristol K5G, APR 423, which was completed by February 1953. Its radiator with two

West Yorkshire Bristol LS5G SMG1 (LWR 431), as modified in 1955 with the CBC intake in the destination box with an out-take louvre on the front roof, and a destination display added below the windscreen. It retained this format until it was withdrawn.

The CBC grilles are either side of the destination display on West Riding 1000 (BHL 351C), one of the last Roe-bodied Guy Wulfrunians built, in service in Bradford. C WARDLEY

grilles was similar to the Southampton Guy test bed and these grilles allowed air to reach the engine air intake and exhaust manifold. It was modified by 1957 to gain a Lodekka concealed front radiator cowl.

Other Tilling companies were also involved with experiments. These included two more Bristol Ks — Crosville K6A FFM 444 new in 1946 and Lincolnshire Road Car GBE 844, a 1950 K5G which initially had an exposed radiator and fluted upper front intakes but was rebuilt in 1958 after an accident and then fitted with a Lodekka cowl.

A United Auto Bristol Lodekka LD6B, 106 BHN new in July 1956, became Tilling's final experimental CBC system, while early production systems went on West Yorkshire Road Car LD6Bs TWY 601-10, UWU 976-8 and UWW739-41 which entered service between October 1957 and November 1958 and had no upper deck opening windows but a mid-front roof air scoop/cowl. Presumably it was thought the CBC system was fully adequate.

The subsequent fitting of grille covers varied the appearance, along with Darvic scoop/grille covers and grille doors; these were to not only direct the air but also to stop excess rain water entering.

There also were Tilling Group trials with Bristol single-deckers. In 1953, West Yorkshire modified two LL5Gs then two years old, JWU 883 in May and JWU 877 in November 1953. The air intake was on the top of the destination indicator, with an out-take vent behind

The company's experiments continued the following year, when a recently withdrawn 1940 L5G, DWW 587, had its bible-type destination display replaced by a radiator, air intake and ventilator assembly. It was not operated in service

but proved the case of how to improve the airflow intake.

Its first underfloor-engined LS5G bus, LWR 431 new in March 1953, had a CBC system fitted by March 1955, with the intake in the destination box and an out-take louvre on the front roof. A small destination indicator was fitted below the windscreen. It remained like this until its normal withdrawal.

Lincolnshire had an LS6G coach, NFW 543, fitted with CBC when delivered in April 1956. It is assumed that with such a radiator placement, the outflow was directed on to the road surface.

Boiling point

A clear advantage of the system was the way its air circulation worked. Conventional floor-mounted heaters just heated up stuffy air that was already inside the bus, but the CBC system allowed the flow of natural air pressure to push fresh air into the bus from the air striking the front. A natural constant intake of fresh air over a radiator/heat exchanger kept the bus fresh and relatively condensation free.

However, as the equipment was not pressurised, if the engine became hot and the water overheated, the water was lost at low revs. On double-deckers, this caused a vertical water fountain from the air vent pipe on the top of a small header tank; this water went over the bonnet top on Lodekkas. A pressurised overflow would have lessened the chance of water being expelled so easily.

With the twin radiator tanks on double-deckers, if the system was heading towards boiling, there was nothing other than the natural air flow to stop this boiling. Drivers were instructed to ensure that radiator vents diverted hot air outside the bus if the temperature gauge read above 200°F.

The absence of a conventional radiator is apparent behind the replaced grille fitted to Cleveland Transit H228 (YAJ 28), a Roe-bodied Leyland Titan PD2/27 new to the Tees-side Railless Traction Board in 1961, in Stockton in May 1974. ALAN MILLAR

Engines get hot and expel water on constant climbs, so with an unfanned and unpressurised system, there was minimal airflow into the CBC vents on a long hill climb. And the first time a bus stopped for any length of time, the low revs on tick over, coupled with a reduced water pumping action, caused water to be expelled in a fountain from the vent from the header tank. This was dangerous for anyone standing nearby.

On most Lodekka FLFs, the CBC tanks had thermostatically-controlled Varivane shutters. These could stick shut (their default position) and, to overcome this, many fleets inserted small rubber bungs. Airflow was then blocked by the shutters when the radiators were warmed and the engine had reached normal temperature, but boiling would result quickly if the vents stayed shut, then boiling would quickly result.

To prevent this, drivers were given such instructions as:

- Ensure that your radiator is kept fully topped up. This must be done with the engine running and preferably when it is warm. Wait for the water to settle before you close the cap. If you fail to do this, it is possible that the system may not be filled completely, and the heater will not work efficiently unless it is.
- Handles in the cab control the air flow separately to lower and upper saloons. For heating purposes pull each handle to the rear to the fullest extent. During warm weather when heating is not required the handles should be fully closed.
- It takes 10min running for the system to warm up so when starting from cold do not pull out the handles immediately otherwise cold air will be circulated which is worse than no heating at all.

- There is a hot air duct fitted in the cab for your comfort. The 'shut' position is clearly marked and in the 'open' position the air stream can be deflected as you wish. The fact that this is working does not necessarily mean that the interior system is working, so check with your conductor at regular intervals.
- If during the day the interior heating becomes less efficient it is probably due to a fall in the water level. Top up at the first opportunity.
- If you have followed these instructions and the heater is still not working, close the handles in the cab and report the fault on the defect sheet. Keep reporting until it is put right.

Buses with CBC systems ran perfectly well for most of the time, but in the view of one person who worked with them, there were weaknesses in its execution. "While it was a common-sense idea, it was fitted badly on Lodekkas," he argues. "Had the units been fitted properly into a sealed casket, they would not have leaked rainwater into the cab, over the driver and the electrics. The result for these poorly fitted units, was wood frame rot to the front bodywork, which in some cases resulted in the cab area and front offside frames requiring a complete rebuild. It is not surprising then that, confronted with such heavy rebuilds, the offending units were removed."

Other installations

The sealed casket he referred to was used on West Riding's Roe-bodied Guy Wulfrunians and they had no reported problems with the CBC equipment, even though many of their other advanced features proved troublesome in the extreme. The CBC system — which West Riding had tested in other double-deckers — was one of the Wulfrunian's essential features, the lack of a radiator in front of the engine helping minimise the amount of space that its large engine occupied on the front platform.

Barton Transport specified CBC in 1960 on six Northern Counties-bodied double-deckers, AEC Regent Vs 850-4 FNN and lowbridge Dennis Loline II 861 HAL, but not on any subsequent deliveries. Significantly, the systems were removed from those six buses.

In the municipal sector, the Tees-side Railless Traction Board had CBC installed in 19 Roe-bodied Leyland Titan PD2/27 and PD2A/27 double-deckers delivered between 1957 and 1967.

Bristol continued to offer CBC as an option on Lodekkas built until 1967, the year before the last examples were built, and although operators including Eastern National and Hants & Dorset continued to take up the option, its practical disadvantages — the unpressurised/unfanned system, the small header tank and poor manual operation — persuaded others to stop using it. Among them was West Yorkshire Road Car, one of the pioneer customers, which removed the equipment from many of its Lodekkas. ∎

Up on the Downs

TERRY BLACKMAN provides a pictorial reminder of some of the vehicles — mostly open-top double-deckers— that took horse race spectators to Epsom Downs between 1983 and 1992 for Derby Day

If you cannot get a seat in the grandstand, what better vantage point is there than upstairs on an open-top double-decker? Among those at Epsom Downs in June 1983 was Eastbourne Borough Council 84 (DHC 784E), a 1967 Leyland Titan PD2A/30 with East Lancs body. The line of double-deckers facing the grandstand includes five of Bournemouth's Alexander-bodied Daimler Fleetlines and two of Merseyside PTE's Weymann-bodied PD2/40s in the red and cream of original owner Southport Corporation.

Champagne was being served aboard Premier Travel's ex-Eastern Counties Bristol Lodekka FLF6G FLF452 (JAH 552D) *Pride of Peterborough* as it transported guests of *Exchange & Mart* magazine in June 1992. Then part of Cambus Holdings' heritage fleet, this bus is privately preserved today.

There are picnic hampers aplenty around two of Southdown's convertible open-top Lodekka FS6Gs, new to Brighton Hove & District in 1960, in June 1983. The rotated National Bus Company logo next to the fleetname commemorated Southdown's success in winning an NBC chairman's award.

One of the farther travelled open-toppers in June 1983 was Lancaster City Council 230 (DBA 230C), a Leyland Atlantean new to Salford Corporation in 1965, which passed into Selnec (later Greater Manchester) PTE ownership in 1969. Lancaster bought five of them in 1978 and converted four to open-top in 1980.

Red Ensign, the coach division of Southampton CityBus, brought this Setra S228DT double-deck coach to Epsom Downs in June 1992. It was one of 34 for UK operators.

LEFT: Bookies offering odds and taking bets in front of some of the line-up in June 1984. The blue and white Leyland Atlantean with Metro-Cammell body was 927 GTA, originally one of Devon General's convertible 'Sea Dogs', new in 1961. It was on loan to Hastings & District from Amalgamated Passenger Transport (APT), the National Bus Company's sales business based near Lincoln. It survives today, having passed through several owners' hands including Stagecoach, First Glasgow and Western Greyhound.

BELOW: Hounslow Coaches turned up in June 1984 with UEL 723, a Bristol Lodekka LD6G new to Hants & Dorset in 1958. It was exported to Sweden to become a burger bar in the 1990s. Behind it is a then brand-new Roe-bodied Leyland Olympian from Bristol Omnibus Company's convertible open-top fleet at Weston-super-Mare.

Strathclyde PTE LA1220 (XUS 591S), an Alexander AL-bodied Leyland Atlantean AN68A/1R new in 1977 and converted to open-top the next year after a deroofing accident, travelled the 400-plus miles from Glasgow for the June 1983 Derby.

The group who hired this Reeve Burgess-bodied Bedford CF from Avon Luxury Coaches put their shoulders and backs into administering the momentum required for a downhill bump start to get them home to Romford.

Two Leyland single-deckers in the Alexander (Fife) fleet in Dumfermline in April 1987. Leyland National 2 FPN32 (YSX 932W) on the right was a 10.6m 44-seater new in January 1981, while FPE175 (NFS 175Y) was one of SBG's last new Leopards, delivered in October 1982 with a dual purpose 49-seat Alexander T-type body. IAIN MacGREGOR

Caledonian choices

DAVID TOY, a former chief engineer at Northern Scottish, explains how the Scottish Bus Group allowed its companies to dictate the specification of the vehicles they bought between 1981 and 1985

Although smaller than the National Bus Company (NBC), the state-owned Scottish Bus Group (SBG) afforded its seven regional subsidiaries more freedom, including their input into specifying vehicles, liveries and, until late 1978, fleetname style.

This reflected how SBG was structured, with four executive directors each having overall day-to-day responsibility for up to two of the subsidiaries. Fifty years ago, three of them were career engineers. One, who retired during 1976, also was the executive director responsible for technical and engineering matters. Roddie MacKenzie had held the post since SBG was transferred in 1969 from the Transport Holding Company (THC) in London to the newly created Scottish Transport Group (STG) in Edinburgh.

While most other board members had worked with the group from leaving school, MacKenzie trained with Edinburgh Corporation, graduated from that city's

university with a degree in engineering and was a municipal general manager in Warrington and Halifax between 1945 and 1956 when he joined SBG as general manager of Scottish Omnibuses, the company better known from 1964 as Eastern Scottish. He was the director in charge of Eastern Scottish and Alexander (Midland).

He was highly influential in SBG's decision to buy bespoke coaches for its predominantly overnight services linking Edinburgh and Glasgow with London, the 12m 42-seat Alexander M-type on rear-engined Bristol REMH6G chassis, but he also held a firm view of the simplicity, versatility and cost-effectiveness that governed its choice of vehicles for urban, interurban and rural services, as SBG was a commercial business that happened to be in state ownership.

His approach was best expressed by SBG's decision to dispose of all 109 of its early model rear-engined Bristol VRT double-deckers, with 106 exchanged with NBC for the same

The first three MCW Metrobuses for Alexander (Midland), including MRM2 (BLS 671V) new in 1979, had a unique version of the lowheight Alexander AD-type body with longer window bays and peaked front and rear roof domes like those on the highbridge AV body on the Volvo Ailsa.
IAIN MacGREGOR

number of forward-entrance front-engined Bristol Lodekka FLF6Gs. Its new vehicle intake was mainly of Alexander-bodied single-deckers with high floors and manual gearboxes — the heavy-duty Leyland Leopard and Seddon Pennine 7 (the latter developed for SBG which wanted the option of a Gardner engine) and lightweight mid-engined Bedford YRQ/YRT and front-engined Ford R-series.

He supported the development of Volvo's front-engined Ailsa double-decker. The prototype ran in public service for the first time in the spring of 1974 with Alexander (Midland), in its blue and cream livery. He had hoped it would simply be an updated Lodekka FLF, and the awkward layout of the solitary lowheight Ailsa (bought by the Derby municipal fleet) limited SBG to buying them for routes and depots that could accommodate highbridge buses.

Daimler (later Leyland) Fleetlines continued to be ordered, but there was no place in MacKenzie's world for the integral Leyland National and he was highly critical of Leyland's plans for its double-deck counterpart, Project B15 which became the Titan, a design in which he detected excessive influence of London Transport and PTEs which relied on public subsidies that SBG did its best to avoid.

MacKenzie's immediate successor, Bob McLeod, had risen over 30 years within SBG from engineering apprentice to chief engineer before becoming a general manager, and was the executive director responsible for Alexander (Northern) and Highland Omnibuses. He went on to become SBG's deputy chairman and his responsibility for engineering passed quickly to an influential newcomer.

A change of direction

Tom Marsden, latterly director of public transportation at Grampian Regional Council, joined the SBG board in February 1976 with responsibility for planning and research. He had been general manager of Aberdeen Corporation Transport from 1964 until the new Grampian council took over in 1975. An engineer in the municipal sector since 1939, he rose through a succession of English undertakings, latterly as general manager at Barrow in Furness.

His engineering influence soon became apparent. Eastern Scottish had a serious vehicle shortage during 1977 caused by the late delivery of Seddons and Fleetlines. He had purchased Leyland Nationals in Aberdeen — the first production 10.3m versions went there in 1973 — and secured ten 11.3m models for Eastern Scottish.

They were judged successful, and 58 more were delivered in 1978 to Central SMT, Alexander (Fife), Alexander (Midland) and Eastern Scottish. Those companies, plus Highland Omnibuses and Alexander (Northern), shared subsequent deliveries of 127 of the slightly longer Leyland National 2 in 1980 and 1981, but the Leyland 680-engined National 2 proved less reliable and no more were bought. Some of the Fife, Midland and Northern vehicles were short wheelbase 10.3m or 10.6m versions.

Most fleets began to specify Leopards and Seddons with semi-automatic gearboxes, only Central continuing with manual gearbox Leopards until 1979.

Six of the seven companies received new Leyland Nationals. Just like City of Oxford at NBC, Western SMT had none. Its executive director also wielded influence. William Sword, educated at private schools in Edinburgh, was the son of Western's founding general

The 1983 order included six Leyland Olympians with Alexander RL bodies for Highland Omnibuses' services in Inverness, which entered service in January 1984, four months before this picture was taken of J3 (A977 OST). IAIN MacGREGOR

manager, whom he succeeded in 1950. He had served an engineering apprenticeship with the company and became executive director solely responsible for Western from 1961, based at its head office in Kilmarnock.

Western sometimes appeared to be semi-detached from SBG and the three unwanted Bristol VRTs not exchanged with NBC for Lodekkas in 1973 were Western ones, sold to dealers on the company's own initiative.

New double-deck designs

Changes also were afoot with double-deckers. SBG ordered three Leyland Titans for Fife in 1977, though in common with many others, it cancelled the order when production delays put the model's future in doubt. Other next generation double-deckers ordered were a Dennis Dominator with lowheight Alexander body for Central in 1978 and three MCW Metrobuses with semi-lowheight Alexander bodies for Midland in 1979.

SBG's requirement for double-deckers was set to grow. Scotmap, based on NBC's Market Analysis Project (MAP), sought to contain increasing operating costs and declining passenger numbers by taking a detailed look at each company's network. Compared with where it stood in 1977, the overall fleet in 1981 was 11.9% smaller, with 494 fewer vehicles. Although the company names did not change until 1985, the corporate fleetname style introduced in late 1978 brought them all into line with Eastern Scottish, as Central Scottish, Fife Scottish, Highland Scottish etc.

SBG's last new Leyland Fleetlines arrived in 1980, with Midland and Western. Double-deck purchases were split four ways thereafter. Direct successor for the Fleetline — and Atlantean and VRT — was the Olympian, the simplified cousin of the Titan.

Among the first Olympians exhibited at the 1980 Motor Show was prototype chassis number four, with ECW body, Gardner 6LXB engine and Leyland's five-speed Hydracyclic gearbox with built in retarder, in Midland Scottish livery. It entered service early in 1981 at the company's Milngavie depot outside Glasgow, its performance measured against one of Midland's three Metrobuses, an Ailsa from Fife and Central's Dominator. The Metrobus and Dominator both had Gardner engines and Voith gearboxes.

The prototype Olympian was transferred to Northern in 1981 and orders for that year were placed for 40 new generation rear-engined double-deckers, all with Alexander RL bodies. There were ten Olympians for Northern, ten Metrobuses for Midland and 20 Dominators for Central. By then, Dennis was producing the Dominator with air suspension and Kirkstall rear axle, but Central specified the earlier model with steel suspension and Dennis drop centre rear axle. Five of them had the 12.2litre Rolls-Royce Eagle engine rated at 180hp in place of the Gardner 6LXB; standard gearbox was the Voith D851, but one had a Maxwell four-speed automatic.

The 1982 order included 21 Olympians with ECW bodies for Northern and 20 for Eastern, the last ECW bodies that SBG bought. Midland took another 30 MCW Metrobuses with Alexander bodies, Central another 20 Dominators, all with Gardner engines. Five of Midland's Metrobuses had Rolls-Royce engines, as did two of its 1981 intake.

Another 46 Olympians, all with Alexander bodies, followed in 1983: 20 for Eastern, ten each for Northern and Fife, and six for Highland. Central and Midland continued with their recent practice, Central with its final ten Dominators to the same specification as before,

SBG moved seamlessly from the front-engined Ailsa to buying Volvo's B10M-based Citybus with horizontal underfloor engine. Eastern Scottish VV169 (B169 KSC), in Edinburgh in August 1987, was one of five delivered in 1985. IAIN MacGREGOR

Five of the six Dennis Lancets for Alexander (Northern) had high-floor Alexander P-type bodies. This is ND5 (A505 FSS) leaving Dundee bus station in May 1984. Similar ND6 is preserved today. IAIN MacGREGOR

Midland with 25 Metrobuses, one with a four-speed Voith gearbox (in place of three-speed) and a revised axle ratio, a trial Tom Marsden initiated to improve fuel consumption.

Western also bought Dominators for the first time, 12 with Alexander bodies, but of the later type with S-cam brakes, Kirkstall hub reduction rear axle and air suspension; two of them had Maxwell gearboxes.

Northern's 1983 Olympians were in a new green and cream Grampian Scottish livery and fitted with Autofare equipment for city services in Aberdeen, which were provided under a single identity with those of Grampian Regional Council. My role as chief engineer there was expanded to hold the same responsibility at Grampian and there was a plan, never enacted, to centralise all engineering at Grampian's King Street site.

By then, Northern had 43 Olympians and serious concerns had arisen on the reliability of the Hydracyclic gearbox. We agreed with Leyland that any future purchases would have Voith transmission, the first four coming in 1984 along with ten with Hydracyclic transmission for Eastern and ten more Metrobuses for Midland. SBG's last of 192 Ailsas arrived in 1984, ten for Eastern and eight for Fife, along with 12 of the new underfloor-engined Volvo Citybus based on the B10M coach.

Two of Fife's Citybuses and two of Eastern's Olympians had long wheelbase chassis and an express coach version of Alexander's R-type body, highbridge RVC on the Volvos and lowheight RLC on the Olympians which had Leyland's TL11 engine in place of the usual Gardner 6LXB. The bodies had a plug-type entrance door, bonded windows and a sliding door covering a luggage area on the nearside entrance.

Orders for 1985, all with Alexander bodies, were for nine Olympians for Highland with 6LXB engines, 13 for Northern (one with a rare Gardner 5LXCT engine), five with TL11 engines for Eastern, 12 more Dominators for Western and five Citybuses for Eastern.

Single-deck options

SBG's last Ford R-series for Highland and Northern were delivered in 1980. It had purchased 427 Fords, with 341 for those two fleets over the previous eight years. They had good fuel consumption, but over time became expensive to maintain with low engine mileage and higher costs on braking components.

To find a more robust lightweight rural bus, two trial buses, with the last Alexander Y-type bodies built, were delivered to Northern in late 1982. One was a front-engined Volvo B57 with the 6.7litre TD70 engine that powered the Ailsa double-decker, the other a mid-engined Dennis Lancet with a Perkins V8 540 engine; both had an Allison automatic gearbox.

The Volvo had one of the lowest Y-type bodies built over the previous 19 years, while the Lancet had one of the highest. The Lancet had better fuel consumption, comparable with the Fords, and another five followed in 1984 with Alexander's new P-type body and air suspension, which made them 3in lower. But the quest for lightweight chassis ended there.

SBG continued to buy Leopards, mainly with Alexander bodies, until 1982, the year after it received the first eight of 311 examples of its successor, the Tiger, which was intended to compete with Volvo's increasingly popular B10M. Leyland exhibited the Tiger chassis at the 1980 Motor Show with its 218hp turbocharged TL11 engine, option of five-speed Pneumo-Cyclic or six-speed ZF manual gearbox, air or steel suspension.

Eastern Scottish took the first eight, with Pneumo-cyclic transmission and air suspension, to start replacing the high mileage M-type Bristols on the Edinburgh-London service, while Western, which had purchased eight Volvo B58s with M-type bodies in 1975, took 12 B10Ms for the Glasgow-London service. All 20 had the new Duple Dominant III body with double-glazed trapezoid windows like those on the M-type, as other

Central SMT's Leyland Tigers with Alexander TS bodies included Gardner-engined LT23 (A23 VDS), new in 1984 and photographed entering Anderston bus station in Glasgow in May 1985. IAIN MacGREGOR

commitments meant that Alexander lacked the time to design a new coach.

A further 21 Tigers and six Volvos with Dominant III bodies were ordered for 1982, ten Tigers for Eastern, seven for Northern and four Tigers and six Volvos for Western after a revision of the group's orders. During the 1982 build the Duple body specification was changed to the high-floor Goldliner design on all but four of the Western Volvos.

The first 11 Tigers for more mundane work, six for Eastern Scottish and five for Central, all with 49-seat dual-purpose Alexander T-type bodies, were delivered in 1982.

Several SBG directors, including William Sword, preferred Gardner engines, a message heeded by Dennis which announced its Dorchester at the 1982 Motor Show, with a choice of 230hp 6HLXCT or 188hp 6HLXB mated to a four-speed Voith automatic gearbox. Western ordered eight of the 6HLXCT version with Plaxton Paramount 3200 coaches bodies for 1983, while Central, with a large single-deck fleet and seeking the best fuel consumption, bought five of the 188hp version which had the same engine/gearbox combination as its Dominators.

Alexander updated its single-deck body designs in 1983, replacing the Y-type with the flat-sided P-type designed for export and the T-type with three new variants, the TS bus, TE express and TC coach. Central's Dorchesters had the TS, as did 10 Tigers which were unusual in having steel suspension and 180hp normally aspirated L11 engines; they had originally been ordered with Y-type bodies to make them even more like the company's Leopards.

In all there were 63 Tigers in 1983. Central also bought five with air suspension, TL11 engines and TE-type bodies, there were 20 for Midland (five each of the last T-types, the first TCs, the TE and Duple Dominant II), three London service Duple Goldliners for Fife, five Dominant IIs and seven P-types on 180hp L11-engined chassis (with air suspension) for Northern, and eight TEs and five Paramount 3200s for Eastern.

The Dorchester spurred Leyland to bow to SBG's request for a Gardner option in the Tiger (180hp 6HLXB and 220hp 6HLXCT) which figured in orders from 1984 onwards. Northern got seven with P-type bodies and 6HLXB engine, which as chief engineer was not my choice; we reverted to TL11 engines on seven Tigers delivered in 1985, five with TC bodies in Scottish Citylink livery and two TEs.

Central bought 20 with 6HLXB engines and TS bodies in 1984 and ordered another 23 for 1985 along with five with 6HLXCT engines and TE bodies. Western bought 20 Plaxton Paramount 3200-bodied Tiger coaches with 6HLXCT engines in 1984 and ordered 15 Dorchesters for 1985 with 6HLXB engines and Paramount 3500 bodies.

Of the other TL11-engined Tigers ordered then, there were ten with 245hp engines for Highland (four with Duple Laser bodies in 1984, six Laser 2s in 1985), 13 for Midland (four Duple Caribbean and six Laser in 1984, three Laser 2 in 1985), 12 with 245hp engines and Plaxton Paramount 3200 bodies for Eastern (three in 1984, nine in 1985) and five with Alexander TC bodies for Fife in 1985.

Western added another 13 Volvo B10M coaches, three with high-floor 60-seat Berkhof Emperor rear saloon bodies, one with a 49-seat Berkhof Esprit body (SBG's first new vehicles with continental European bodies) and nine with Plaxton Paramount 3500 bodies. The first Esprit arrived in 1984, the others in 1985.

Power from behind

SBG also began to buy rear-engined coaches, the first since the last of the 70 M-type Bristols in 1971. When MCW launched the double-deck Metroliner (based on the three-axle Metrobus chassis) at the October 1982 Motor Show, the prototype was in a striking SBG livery and was intended for Northern. It was powered by a Cummins L10 engine rated at 290hp, matched to a Voith automatic gearbox; the interior, in standard group coach colours, had 69 reclining seats, a rear toilet and a large luggage area behind the rearmost axle with access doors on both sides. Seven more followed in 1984 for London services, three each for Eastern and Western, a second one for Northern.

Four of the original 3.2m high single-deck Metroliner followed late in 1984, two each for Eastern and Northern. They had a 250hp L10 engine with a Self Changing Gears Hydracyclic gearbox. Northern's two were for the Aberdeen-London service and the new 600mile Aberdeen-Plymouth route operated in conjunction with National Express, then the longest express service in the country; it was extended later to Penzance. We soon found that the failure rate of the Hydracyclic gearbox was unacceptable, and the coaches were returned to MCW to fit a Voith transmission.

Also ordered in late 1982 for 1983 delivery were six Leyland Royal Tiger Doyens with TL11 engines, two each for Eastern, Northern and Western. Eastern and Northern specified the five-speed Hydracyclic gearbox, Western a six-speed ZF manual. They had 46 Fuglesang Miami reclining seats with an adjustable headrest, and a rear toilet. Build problems at Roe delayed their delivery until 1984 and they were the last to carry SBG's blue and white London livery introduced in 1976. Willian Sword disliked them and had the Western pair reallocated to Fife.

A major restructure

Our world was about to change in preparation for deregulation in October 1986. In December 1984, SBG's board directors informed the seven subsidiaries' management teams that a reorganisation would create four new operating companies, to be formed in March 1985 and operated from June. Five of the seven central works would transfer to a new commercial company, SBG Engineering, and Scottish Citylink Coaches took over the management of most express services.

The new companies were Clydeside (from Western), Kelvin (from Midland, Eastern and Central), Strathtay (from Northern and Midland) and Lowland (from Eastern). All 11 were named in a standard style, e.g. Clydeside Scottish Omnibuses. Some vehicles ordered for 1985 were delivered to the new companies.

New vehicles, minibuses as well as single- and double-deckers and coaches, were ordered for 1986 and 1987, and in much smaller quantities afterwards, augmented by ex-London Routemasters for a reintroduction of crew operation by three of the companies. It was announced in 1988 that SBG was to be privatised and the subsidiaries, reduced again from 11 area companies to nine, were sold in 1990 and 1991. ∎

Western SMT M162 (A162 TGE), a four-month-old 69-seat MCW Metroliner, loading in Hamilton in August 1984 on a fast daytime Glasgow-London service. Alongside it is a ten-year-old Central SMT Leyland Leopard with 53-seat Alexander Y-type body, one of 384 bought new between 1964 and 1982. IAIN MacGREGOR

The driver and conductor stand in Bakewell Square alongside Hulley's 24 (FA 9100), a rear-entrance Guy-bodied Guy Arab III new to Burton upon Trent Corporation in 1948, ready to depart on service 1 to Middleton by Youlgrave. PETER ROBERTS

Hulleys of Baslow

JOHN YOUNG relates the story of one of the last operators to survive in independent hands from the birth of mass bus operation in the early 1920s

When Hulleys of Baslow ceased trading in March 2025, the Derbyshire operator was one of the last independents surviving from the pioneering days of motorbus operation after World War One.

Its founder, taxi proprietor Henry Hulley, then nearly 48, bought his first bus, a 14-seat Ford Model T, in April 1921 for a service connecting Baslow, where he was landlord of the Rutland Arms Hotel, with Chesterfield via Freebirch, Cutthorpe and Newbold. He also had a family home built opposite the hotel, with a garage and yard for the fleet to expand, a facility that remained right to the end.

Those were highly competitive times and Hulley re-routed most of his journeys via Wadshelf and Old Brampton in September 1922, with some extended back from Baslow to start from Bakewell via Pilsley, thus establishing the core of what latterly was route 170. He was operating on Mondays, Thursdays and Saturdays by November that year, daily from April 1923. A second route, connecting Bakewell, Youlgrave and Middleton-by-Youlgrave began in 1925, with some journeys extended to Chesterfield.

A new daily service between Baslow and Tideswell in June 1930 competed between Baslow and Eyam with one

licensed a fortnight earlier to his nephew, Stan Eades, between Chesterfield, Baslow and Eyam. Eades joined his uncle's business when it took over the licence six months later. Hulley's route now ran between Chesterfield, Baslow, Calver and Eyam to Tideswell.

When the 1930 Road Traffic Act took effect, Hulley secured road service licences in 1931 for all three of its routes, Chesterfield-Bakewell-Middleton, Chesterfield-Tideswell and Chesterfield-Freebirch, the last of which was authorised to operate on Mondays as well as Saturdays. Excursion licences included such destinations as Alton Towers, Blackpool, Skegness, Southport and York.

With seven buses owned by then, fleetnumbers 1 to 7 were allocated for the first time in 1934. When a vehicle was withdrawn, its replacement took that number, a policy that applied for most of the company's existence. Superstition dictated that number 13, on an AEC Regal withdrawn in 1957, did not reappear until 2020.

To secure the future of the business as he wished to retire, Henry Hulley formed a limited company, Henry Hulley & Sons, in January 1938; shares were divided among family members, but he retained the majority. He died in June 1955.

Hulley's first underfloor-engined vehicle was 11 (MWJ 197), a Windover-bodied AEC Regal IV new to Sheffield United Tours in 1950, purchased in March 1959. Here, the central-entrance coach loads in Chesterfield. PETER ROBERTS

Few secondhand underfloor-engined single-deck service buses were available in the early 1960s when Hulley's bought ex-Midland Red BMMOs including 19 (LHA 400), a Brush-bodied S9 new in 1949. It was in Baslow, crossing the River Derwent by the Rutland Arms where Henry Hulley once was the landlord. PETER ROBERTS

Two routes of another family business, Maurice Kenyon, were acquired in May 1939 along with two vehicles. These were a daily service between Baslow, Calver and Grindleford station, connecting with trains from Sheffield and Manchester, and a Mondays-only market day run between Grindleford and Bakewell via Calver and Stoney Middleton.

Postwar developments
One of Hulleys' first postwar moves, in June 1946, was to acquire the services of Sellers & Kent, trading as The Green Bus Service. Its main route linked Ilam with Ashbourne via Dovedale, Thorpe and Mappleton, supplemented by a Wednesdays-only market day service to Leek.

The network was large enough to introduce route numbers in 1948, 1 (Chesterfield-Baslow-Bakewell-Middleton), 2 (Chesterfield-Baslow-Eyam-Tideswell), 3 (Chesterfield-Cutthorpe-Freebirch), 4 (Baslow-Grindleford station), 5 (Grindleford-Eyam-Bakewell), 6 (Ashbourne-Mappleton-Thorpe-Ilam), 7 (Ilam-Leek) and 8 (Ashbourne-Mappleton-Blor-Ilam). The 3 was extended later beyond Chesterfield to Baslow once again.

The fleet reached its maximum of 28 vehicles in 1950. In the winter only 14 buses were required for the stage services. The summer coach fleet included a Duple-bodied AEC Regal II delivered in May 1947, the first new vehicle for nine years.

To reduce costs on routes 6, 7 and 8, a Roe-bodied Bedford OWB utility bus, new in 1943 to Bullock's of Featherstone, was bought in 1952 and converted for one-man operation by reducing its seating capacity. The OWB and the three routes were sold to Warrington's of Ilam at the end of 1954.

Yeates Europa-bodied Bedford SB5 1 (2626 UP), with chassis converted by the Loughborough coachbuilder to door forward layout, in Bakewell Square. It was new to Armstrong's of Ebchester in 1962. PETER ROBERTS

Strachans-bodied Ford R226 4 (NPM 315F) was new to Evan Evans Tours in London in 1968, one 26 R226s and shorter R192s sold after Wallace Arnold acquired that business early in 1969. PETER YEOMANS

One of the ex-Liverpool MCW-bodied Leyland Panthers acquired ex-Merseyside PTE, 43 (FKF 922F). TONY WILSON

A new route 6 introduced on Whit Sunday 1956 was a long time coming. In June 1939, at the request of the Ramblers Association, Hulleys applied to extend some Sunday journeys beyond Middleton via Friden and Newhaven to Hartington, a popular starting point for hikers. The 6 followed the same timings as proposed 17 years earlier and connected at Baslow with Sheffield Joint Omnibus Committee service 37 (Sheffield-Bakewell), providing Sheffield and Chesterfield ramblers with convenient access to the Dovedale and Manifold Valleys.

Hulleys had failed to obtain licences for other new routes in 1947 and 1950, including Bakewell-Castleton and Chesterfield-Buxton connections, as it was nigh on impossible to win in a road service licensing system that protected existing services.

The livery was simplified in the 1950s to red and cream, from red below the windows with a duck egg grey roof and window pillars, maroon band between the red and grey and maroon wheelarches.

Notable additions to the fleet were a new Duple Vega-bodied Bedford SBG coach delivered in May 1957 in memory of Henry Hulley, and a Windover-bodied AEC Regal IV in March 1959, its first underfloor-engined vehicle, new to Sheffield United Tours in November 1950. Hulleys also bought five of Midland Red's early underfloor-engined single-deckers, BMMO type S8 and S9, in the early 1960s.

Change of ownership

Like many others, Hulleys became locked in a cycle of falling patronage, rising costs and fares. It reduced services and the original route, 3 (Baslow-Chesterfield via Freebirch), ended in July 1970, carrying so few passengers that the company's car operated the final journey. The peak vehicle requirement fell then to 11.

It added two routes in 1971, filling gaps created when North Western Road Car cut back. The 11 (Bakewell-Over Haddon) started in January with six round trips a day,

Silver Service 65 (AML 569H), the ex-London Transport AEC Merlin with MCW body, at Darley Dale. TONY WILSON

The Bristol REs included Silver Service 64 (JEH 184K), an ECW-bodied RESL6L new to Potteries in 1971 and photographed in Bakewell in July 1983. TONY WILSON

Bristol REs sourced from Trent included 1974 ECW coach-bodied RELH6L 16 (YCH 896M) photographed at Windmill, near Great Hucklow on a summer leisure service in May 1989. JOHN YOUNG

followed in December by the school times and Saturdays 12 (Bakewell-Great Longstone-Monsal Head).

The family business also was running out of family and sought a new owner. Of the second generation, Thomas Hulley died in April 1971, the other three directors, Jack, Ben and Nina, were nearing retirement and none of the third generation were interested in running buses. Jack and Nina lived another 20 years, until August 1993 and December 1995 respectively.

East Midland and Trent expressed interest in acquiring some of Hulleys routes, but not the company. Chesterfield Transport bid to purchase the whole concern in 1976, but the council withdrew its offer in May 1977.

It was finally sold in August 1978 to JH Woolliscroft & Son, trading as Silver Service, of Darley Dale. Only ten of Hulleys' buses were licensed, with some in poor condition. One of the new owner's first moves was to introduce double-deckers, acquiring five former Western SMT Bristol Lodekka FLF6Gs, allocating two each to Baslow and Darley Dale and stripping the fifth for spares. The two fleets were numbered into one series and, when a new bus arrived, it received the next consecutive number, instead of the Hulleys system of filling gaps left by withdrawn vehicles.

One product of the takeover, implemented a year later in September 1979, was to link Hulleys' service 1 (Chesterfield-Bakewell) with the Silver Service route between Bakewell and Matlock via Stanton and Winster and renumbering it 170, while new service 171 linked Bakewell and Middleton-by-Youlgrave. The 170 was shared by red and honey buses from Baslow and blue and honey ones from Darley Dale.

By spring 1979, a familiar figure and future owner was assistant traffic manager of the combined business. Peter Eades, born 1938, had worked for Hulleys since 1961 as a fitter and later a driver. His uncle Stan was a nephew of Henry Hulley. His appointment was short-lived, and he returned to driving, as disagreements between the directors of Silver Service led to the Baslow and Darley Dale operations being managed separately.

Panthers and REs
Desperate for newer vehicles, a leasing business offered 15 former Merseyside PTE Leyland Panthers, with an arrangement for a company at Leabrooks, near Alfreton, to maintain them. Only seven were acquired, the deal having been agreed without realising that the Panthers were too

Also from Trent but new to South Wales Transport was 20 (OCY 907R), the ECW-bodied Bristol VRT/SL3 acquired in 1994 for school peaks. TONY WILSON

The fleet in March 1997 included 14 (Q364 FVT), a 1970 Leyland Leopard with a 1992-built Willowbrook Warrior body. This was its third body, as it originally was a Plaxton Panorama Elite coach with Hebble, registered LJX 817H. A subsequent owner fitted it with a Duple Dominant body from a Bedford YMT coach. The Willowbrook body was fitted when it was owned by Border Buses of Burnley. TONY WILSON

Former Nottingham City Transport Leyland National 2s, including 19 (RRA 218X), retained their South Notts colours and introduced a new fleet livery. TONY WILSON

long and low for Peak District roads. Breakdowns were frequent, and repairs were often slow and of poor quality.

There was talk in early 1980 of purchasing of up to 14 Plaxton Derwent-bodied Ford R-series from Midland Red. Only four were bought, two each for Baslow and Darley Dale. Their small engines struggled with the hills.

An ex-Glasgow Leyland Atlantean and two ex-Nottingham Daimler Fleetlines replaced the Lodekkas in August 1980 and more rear-engined single-deckers — an ex-London Transport AEC Merlin and two ex-Potteries Bristol RESLs — followed in 1981. But another crisis required drastic action.

The Baslow garage, being rebuilt over the 1981/82 winter to accommodate taller vehicles, became unusable after inspection pits flooded and froze. The fleet was in a poor state when ministry examiners carried out an inspection in February 1982, issuing every vehicle except the two ex-Nottingham Fleetlines with prohibition notices; that prompted a traffic commissioners' hearing the following month and a subsequent licence reduction, but services were maintained.

The worst buses were withdrawn and Chesterfield Transport, East Midland and later Barton loaned buses to Hulleys. Core service 170 (Chesterfield-Matlock) was moved to the Darley Dale base using Silver Service licences and buses, with Baslow covering less frequent village runs. The Hulley fleetname disappeared for a while, although the buses at Baslow were still licensed to Henry Hulley & Sons and carried that title on the legal lettering.

Former service 12 (Bakewell-Monsal Head), by then 173, was taken over by Andrew's of Tideswell from April 1982; the same Andrew's that took over most of Hulleys' routes when the company closed in 2025.

Salvation came with 13 Bristol REs purchased in 1982/83 — one with an ECW body from East Midland, six Northern

Counties-bodied and four Pennine-bodied from Burnley & Pendle, and two ex-Ribble RESL6Ls with Marshall bodywork. One Panther escaped the ministry inspection by being off-site and was the only one painted in Silver Service blue and honey. It outlived the other six but was withdrawn in 1983 along with the last Fords.

Operations at Baslow and Darley Dale were combined at the start of 1983, with drivers and buses from both depots working the same duties and covering all routes.

Route developments

The September 1979 route renumbering, which Derbyshire County Council introduced to eliminate duplication, also changed the 2 (Chesterfield-Tideswell) to 172, the 4 (Grindleford-Bakewell) to 174, 5 (Eyam-Bakewell) to 175, 6 (Chesterfield-Hartington) to 176, 13 (Bakewell-Monyash) to 177, 11 (Bakewell-Over Haddon) to 178, and 14 (Baslow-Beeley) to 179.

The 173 (Bakewell-Monsal Head) was extended to Tideswell via Wardlow in September 1981, linked to the 172 so that buses ran from Chesterfield via Eyam to Tideswell and continued to Bakewell as the 173. New route 182, introduced two months later, provided two Saturday journeys from Castleton to Chesterfield to bring Hope Valley residents to the new Pavements shopping centre.

The annual Bakewell Show generated additional revenue for the company and the Peak Park Planning Board invited Hulleys to provide a park-&-ride service in 1984 using the old railway trackbed between Hassop and Bakewell along part of the Monsal Trail walking route. This unusual arrangement continued until 2017.

Hulleys' horizons widened in January 1985 when it accompanied two National Bus Company (NBC) subsidiaries on the two-hourly Lincman connecting

Wright Eclipse Urban-bodied Volvo B7RLE 25 (MX55 UAA), ex-First Manchester, heading for Manchester Airport on route X57 on the Snake Pass in May 2021. JOHN YOUNG

Manchester and Lincoln. The initiative came from NBC's East Midland, which teamed up with Lincolnshire Road Car to extend service X67 (Manchester-Mansfield) to Lincoln. It provided three of the five vehicles, Hulleys and Lincolnshire one each. Hulleys' was a Leyland Leopard purchased from Clyde Coast with a Plaxton Supreme IV body; it was branded for the X67.

All local bus work was concentrated then at Baslow, with Darley Dale looking after coaching and contracts. The other 11 buses at Baslow were Bristol REs.

In preparation for deregulation in October 1986, Hulley's registered hourly timetables on the 170 (Chesterfield-Bakewell-Youlgrave-Matlock) and 178 (Bakewell-Shutts Lane), two journeys on the 171 (Bakewell-Youlgrave) and some Bakewell Monday market day runs on 175 (Eyam-Bakewell), 177 (Monyash-Bakewell) and 179 (Bakewell-Birchover-Rowsley-Chatsworth-Bakewell circular).

Tendered work gained included Bakewell to Over Haddon, with two journeys extended via the narrow Conksbury Bridge to Youlgrave and Middleton, and the 181 from Dronfield to Hartington and Buxton, returning via Castleton. Route 173 (Bakewell-Tideswell), which passed from Andrew's to Trent, was won back in July 1987 along with Trent route 197, with one return journey between Castleton and Buxton via Tideswell three days a week.

Another tendering gain, in July 1987, was of Matlock area services 64 (Clay Cross), 158 (Starkholmes) and 160 (Hackney) which prompted the purchase the next month of a 25-seat MCW Metrorider, the first new vehicle to carry Hulleys legal lettering since 1957 and its first new service bus since 1936.

There were losses, too. Sunday service 170 journeys passed to East Midland in 1986. Whites of Calver won the next contract in September 1992, but Hulleys won it back

again in April 2000 by which time Whites was owned by Chesterfield Transport.

The X67 was cut back from Lincoln to Mansfield July 1987, but two journeys were extended from Manchester to Liverpool; it was then operated only by East Midland and Hulleys, with one vehicle from each. By 1988, it only served Liverpool on Mondays, Fridays and Saturdays. Hulleys' involvement ended in October 1998 when, reduced to a one-bus operation, the contract was awarded to Ringwood Coaches of Chesterfield.

The late 1986 arrival of three Wadham Stringer-bodied Bedford YMTs from Maidstone heralded a new livery of larkspur blue and white with Hulleys Services fleetnames in white, soon applied to other vehicles including two ECW-bodied Bristol RELHs purchased ex-Trent in December 1987.

Separate again

When the Woolliscrofts offered Hulleys for sale in 1988, some drivers at Baslow tried to arrange an employee buy-out but it was sold to traffic manager Arthur Cotterill and long-serving employee and Hulley relative Peter Eades, who took control on New Year's Day 1989 and completed the deal on March 31. Silver Service retained the Matlock minibus contract, for which the Metrorider transferred to Darley Dale in November 1988, but that business went into receivership in February 1990.

A shelf company, Hovercroft, was renamed Henry Hulley & Sons, all 14 buses — seven Bristol REs, four Bedfords and single examples of Ford, AEC Reliance and Leyland Leopard — carried the fleetname Hulleys of Baslow and retained the blue and white livery. Once again, buses were numbered from 1 upwards (omitting the unlucky 13) with newcomers allocated the identities of recently withdrawn vehicles.

As part of Hulleys' centenary celebration, Alexander Dennis Enviro200 was painted in North Western Road Car heritage livery.
RUSSELL YOUNG

Hulleys' services reached Sheffield for the first time in January 1989 when it took over Trent's share of route 272 (Sheffield-Castleton); some journeys were extended to Meadowhall when the retail complex opened in September 1990.

Hulleys turned down a takeover bid from Trent in July 1991. By then it was running coaches again, on private hires, excursions and holidays, and by January 1994 the 18-strong fleet was made up of coaches and coach-seated buses. There were nine Leyland Leopards, four Leyland Tigers, three Bedford YNTs, one Volvo B10M and a Mercedes-Benz 609D minibus. Four of the trusty Bristol REs had survived into 1992 and the last was withdrawn in July 1993.

Capacity rather than comfort was the requirement of an acquisition in April 1994, a 77-seat ECW-bodied Bristol VRT/SL3 double-decker from Trent to cater for school journeys on service 170; it was new 17 years earlier to South Wales Transport. The purchase of another ECW-bodied double-decker brought a change of livery. The Leyland Fleetline retained the dark blue and cream of former owner South Notts, as did some Leyland National 2s that followed it, and that became the new bus livery.

Coaches remained blue and white, including a Plaxton Premiere-bodied Dennis Javelin delivered in January 1998, Hulleys' first new coach since 1957. Within eight years, however, coach work had declined, and they were gradually replaced by buses, some with seatbelts for short private hires, and the last coach departed in November 2019.

After the Leyland National 2, the Leyland Lynx found favour, with seven acquired from various sources. Three Optare Sigma-bodied Dennis Lances came from Trent in 2004; withdrawal of the last of these ten years later ended step-entrance bus operation and Hulleys' use of roller destination blinds.

New buses galore

Until 2005, Hulleys had only purchased two new service buses, a Park Royal-bodied AEC Regal in 1936 and the Metrorider in 1987. That changed with the arrival of two 40-seat MCV Evolution-bodied MAN 14.220s in April and September 2005, joined in 2008 by an MAN 12.240 with 37-seat Plaxton Centro body. Two Optare Solos were delivered in 2006, a 27-seat M880SL in March and a 28-seat M850SL in October, followed in 2009 by a 28-seat M880SL.

A 37-seat Alexander Dennis Enviro200 arrived in time for Hulleys' 90th anniversary in April 2011; many secondhand examples came afterwards. Seven of the 19 vehicles owned in July 2014 were bought new, an all-time record.

Tendered service gains from TM Travel in October 2011 increased Hulleys' presence in Sheffield, requiring a double-decker again after 11 years. An Alexander ALX400-bodied Volvo B7TL was followed two years later by a similar Dennis Trident. The fleet became all single-deck again in January 2018.

Hulleys had faced its only direct competition from March 1994 when Bakewell Coaches began three local services using a Freight Rover Sherpa minibus. It responded seven weeks later with three of its own local services, numbered 1, 2 and 3, using a Mercedes-Benz 609D with Bakewell Omnibus fleetname.

Bakewell Coaches stepped things up in February 1996 with new service 150 (Moorhall Estate-Bakewell-Chesterfield-Royal Hospital) challenging Hulleys' 170, but it ended two months later when Hulleys acquired the Bakewell town services and the Sherpa minibus.

The main trunk routes were renumbered in October 1998, with 170 becoming Chesterfield-Bakewell-Shutts Lane/Over Haddon, 171 Bakewell-Youlgrave-Middleton

The final Hulleys' livery on 22 (LK57 AYB), an Alexander Dennis Enviro400, in the village of Eyam on service 257 to Sheffield.
JOHN YOUNG

and 172 the original Silver Service Bakewell-Matlock route via the villages.

Another seasonal tender win, in 2006, was for scenic and demanding route 260 (Castleton-Edale), which the Peak Park Planning Board withdrew five years later and awarded Hulleys service 222 from Derwent, Fearfall Wood using its private road passing Derwent and Howden reservoirs to Kings Tree. Late evening runs on most routes were withdrawn then.

Hulleys returned to Ashbourne in October 2019, awarded contracts for rural services 110/111 (Matlock-Ashbourne) following the sudden closure of Your Bus.

The last brave blast

Peter Eades became sole owner in July 2001, and his 43-year-old son Richard joined the business as a co-director, when Arthur Cotterill, then 62, left the company. Richard Eades became managing director when his father died in July 2013, with his mother Muriel as a co-director. The final chapter of Hulleys' long story began when he stepped down as MD in September 2019 and sold the business to his successor, former Hulleys driver Alf Crofts, in March 2020.

Crofts, four years older than Richard Eades, was quick to make his mark, repainting buses, replacing the oldest with newer secondhand stock and introducing an updated fleetname and strapline 'Proudly serving the Peak District since 1921'. A brave move in November 2019 added new commercial service X70, direct via the A619 between Bakewell and Chesterfield to offer a 30min combined frequency with the 170.

Also added were a seasonal weekend service to Alton Towers, the X57 between Sheffield, Manchester and Manchester Airport via the Snake Pass and – for three days only – a linked extension numbered X1 from the airport via Macclesfield and Leek to Ashbourne. New Transmach ticket machines enabled contactless payments.

When Hulleys celebrated its centenary in April 2021, it did so in style. Once again, a new bus marked the occasion. MCV EvoRa-bodied Volvo B8RLE 21 (Y100 HOB) was the first of two, the second arriving in August 2023. Several vehicles were painted in past operators' liveries, including Silver Service and North Western, and an Enviro200 was decked out in Hulleys' historic red and cream.

There were frequent network and fleet changes. More double-deckers — Alexander Dennis Enviro400s — arrived. Marginal services run previously by Stagecoach were adopted commercially, taking Hulleys as far afield as Alfreton and Killamarsh. It also expanded a long way from home, acquiring the 30-vehicle Go-Coach business in Swanley, Kent which provided in-house engineering services. Go-Coach's livery is yellow and purple, prompting a change of Hulleys' colours to blue and yellow. Five new 40-seat Enviro200 MMCs were delivered in 2023/24.

Gradually cracks appeared: service delivery deteriorated, customer confidence disappeared, Go-Coach was reacquired by its former owner and the newest Enviro200s returned to their leasing company. The business was in financial difficulty and contemplated closing at the end of 2024.

It survived until March 2025, a sad end to 104 years of serving local communities. Andrew's of Tideswell took over most routes and 14 of the 17 vehicles (Solos, Enviro200s and Enviro400s). The Volvo B8RLEs and an Enviro200 went to Connexions Buses in Yorkshire, which had been assisting Hulleys in its final weeks. ∎

Halfcabs on the 83

LES DICKINSON remembers the double-deckers of his childhood in suburban Sheffield

I was a young boy in 1952 when my family moved to a new council house on the Birley estate alongside the prewar Frecheville district, much of which straddled the Birley Moor Road, served by four routes of the Sheffield Joint Omnibus Committee (JOC) B fleet.

This was Derbyshire then, as the Sheffield boundary was at Intake tram terminus. Other operators ran there too, but with restrictions within the city boundary. East Midland's 3 from Mansfield, in superb chocolate, biscuit and cream, was joined later by Chesterfield Corporation's dark green and cream on a joint service with the JOC.

As Birley grew, it got its own JOC service 83 from Pond Street bus station, routed via the equally new Base Green estate, terminating at a junction with Birley Lane which today is on the Supertram line to Crystal Peaks. B fleet buses showed Sheffield rather than City on their destination blinds and those on the 83 were provided by Leadmill Road garage.

My memory is of a half-hourly frequency on Sundays and late evenings, 20min through the working day and

A 1948 all-Leyland Titan PD2/1, 34 (KWB 834), on the 83. JS COCKSHOTT ARCHIVE

15min on Saturdays, with the whole journey taking about 25min, and a requirement for two, three or four double-deckers. There also were rush hour duplicates, some of

Sheffield JOC 2123 (LWA 23), a Roberts-bodied AEC Regent III new in November 1948, waiting to depart from Pond Street bus station on the 83 to Birley. SOUTH YORKSHIRE TRANSPORT MUSEUM

ECW-bodied Leyland Titan PD2/20 1294 (YWB 294). The bodies on this unique quintet resembled those on highbridge Bristol KSWs. ROY MARSHALL/THE BUS ARCHIVE

them shorts to Base Green which loaded and departed Pond Street ahead of those for Birley.

The regular performers were all-Leyland Titan PD2/1s and Roberts-bodied AEC Regent IIIs new in 1948 and Roe-bodied Regent IIIs new in 1952. The Weymann-bodied PD2/12s of 1953 were new after we moved in, but all these looked old fashioned after concealed radiator Regent IIIs with Roe bodies arrived in 1955. Sheffield's Roe-bodied double-deckers often had blue window surrounds, but these also had blue fronts.

They were joined in 1957 by consecutively numbered 1294/5, both Leyland Titan PD2/20s but not peas in a pod. The more unusual was 1294, one of five of this unique combination in Sheffield with ECW bodies.

Roe-bodied 1295 was the more comfortable, if less interesting of the pair.

Buses alternated day about between those with odd and even fleetnumbers. Two of the extra buses introduced at tea time remained in service for the evening, while those that had been there all day retired to the garage.

When 30ft Roe-bodied Regent Vs arrived in 1960, they operated the 83 on Sundays, later also on Saturdays. Our first rear-engined buses were Park Royal-bodied Daimler Fleetlines which entered service on a Friday evening of the first week of January 1965. My ride to the Scouts meeting on City Road had never been so good as on that brand new bus. The downside was that the halfcab days were numbered. ∎

The Leyland body on 13 (LWE 213), a 1949 Titan PD2/1, was of the Farington design, with separately mounted window vents. JS COCKSHOTT ARCHIVE

Sheffield's last AEC Regent IIIs, delivered in 1955, had concealed radiators and bonnet assemblies more common on the then newly introduced Regent V. The grille surround of Roe-bodied 1263 (UWE 763) was painted blue. On the right is 82 (HWB 382), a 1945 Daimler CWA6 with Duple wartime utility body. JS COCKSHOTT ARCHIVE

SUBSCRIBE TODAY!

WHICH *BUSES MAGAZINE* SUBSCRIPTION SUITS YOU BEST?

A 12 MONTH SUBSCRIPTION *BEST VALUE*

UK PRINT - 1 year

£56.99

Paying by Annual Direct Debit

PLUS A FREE GIFT!

B 6 MONTH SUBSCRIPTION

UK PRINT - 6 months

£29.00

Paying by 6-month Direct Debit

PLUS A FREE GIFT!

FREE GIFT

BUSES YEARBOOK 2025 (BOOKZINE)

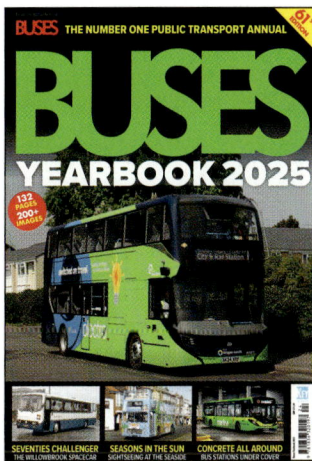

WORTH £11.99!

The softback version of the popular *Buses Yearbook 2025* follows a proven format with a mixture of articles on current and historic developments, strictly factual ones, and others of a more whimsical or personal nature, all of them accompanied by a wide selection of photographs.

The present-day content includes the introduction of electric buses in Oxford and London, the growing number of buses and coaches imported from China.

BUSES THE NUMBER ONE PUBLIC TRANSPORT ANNUAL

BUSES YEARBOOK 2025

132 PAGES
200+ IMAGES

SEVENTIES CHALLENGER THE WILLOWBROOK SPACECAR

SEASONS IN THE SUN SIGHTSEEING AT THE SEASIDE

CONCRETE ALL AROUND BUS STATIONS UNDER COVER

READER REVIEW* - ★★★★★

"Excellent for anyone interested in London's Transport system over the years.— 5 star Interesting and informative."

READER REVIEW *- ★★★★★

"A very good magazine. Excellent articles and the fleet news is exceptional."

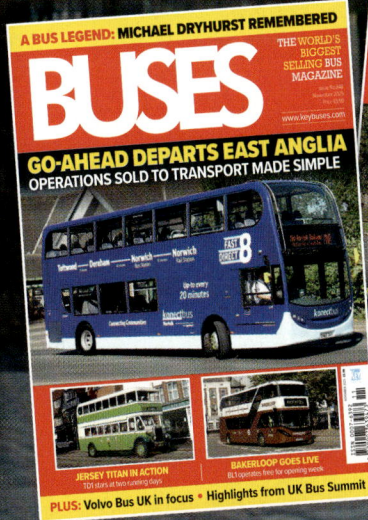

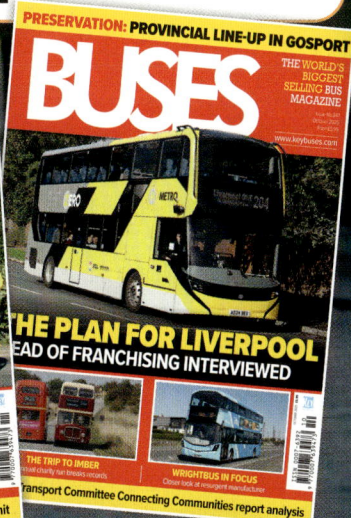

A BUS LEGEND: MICHAEL DRYHURST REMEMBERED

BUSES THE WORLD'S BIGGEST SELLING BUS MAGAZINE

GO-AHEAD DEPARTS EAST ANGLIA OPERATIONS SOLD TO TRANSPORT MADE SIMPLE

JERSEY TITAN IN ACTION TD 1 stars at two cruising days

BAKERLOOP GOES LIVE BL1 operates time for opening week

PLUS: Volvo Bus UK in focus • Highlights from UK Bus Summit

PRESERVATION: PROVINCIAL LINE-UP IN GOSPORT

BUSES THE WORLD'S BIGGEST SELLING BUS MAGAZINE

THE PLAN FOR LIVERPOOL HEAD OF FRANCHISING INTERVIEWED

THE TRIP TO IMBER Small charity run threatens records

WRIGHTBUS IN FOCUS Closer look at emergent manufacturer

Transport Committee Connecting Communities report analysis

*Reader reviews from Pocketmags

REASONS TO SUBSCRIBE TO *BUSES* MAGAZINE...

» **EXCLUSIVE** Subscriber offers on the *Key Publishing* Shop   » **SAVE** over buying individual issues
» **DELIVERED DIRECT** to your door   » **BE THE FIRST** to read the latest features
» **SUBSCRIBER DISCOUNTS** on *Key Publishing* event tickets

SCAN HERE TO SUBSCRIBE TODAY!

BorderBus operates a network of services radiating from its base in Beccles to Norwich, Great Yarmouth, Bungay, Halesworth, Southwold and Aldeburgh. The fleet mainly comprises Alexander Dennis Enviro200s and Scania OmniCity double-deckers. Vehicles bought new include an Alexander Dennis Enviro400 MMC and this MCV EvoRa-bodied Volvo B8RLE, 113 (BB73 BUS), pictured departing Norwich on service 146 to Beccles, Kessingland and Southwold.

Time to head east again

MARK BAILEY shows some recent developments in Norfolk, Suffolk, Lincolnshire and Cambridgeshire

Enticed by reading in *Buses* about recent developments in the east of England, I decided it was time to pay another visit to see them for myself.

Changes at First Bus Eastern Counties include renewal and rebranding of its seasonal open-top services in and around Great Yarmouth. New buses had been added to the fleets of several independents, such as Sanders, Lynx, Coach Services, BorderBus and Dews, and Vectare had acquired Simonds.

And there had been changes in and around Cambridge since my last visit, including the introduction of electric buses.

A holiday in Norfolk, north Suffolk and the Lincolnshire and Cambridgeshire fens in August 2024 provided the ideal opportunity to combine sightseeing in this attractive part of the country with photographing and sampling the local transport scene. ■

Boston-based Brylaine has over 60 vehicles, made up of Optare Solos and Tempos, Alexander ALX400-bodied Dennis Tridents and Wright-bodied Volvo double-deckers. Destinations include Lincoln, Horncastle, Spilsby, Mablethorpe, Skegness and Spalding. Seen passing Boston Market Place with St Botolph's Church behind is smartly-repainted Volvo B9TL/Wright Eclipse Gemini 214 (X25 XBT) working service B9 to Spalding. It was new to First Manchester as MX07 BVD.

Unique in England, Stagecoach East operates 12 tri-axle Volvo B8Ls with 98-seat two-door Alexander Dennis Enviro400XLB bodywork. They are deployed on service B linking Hinchingbrooke Hospital via Huntingdon, St Ives and the Cambridgeshire guided busway with Cambridge city centre, where 13911 (BU69 XYM) is pictured arriving. The guided busway opened in 2011 and is the longest in the world.

Vectare acquired the long-established Simonds of Diss in May 2024. Operations remain separate, albeit within the Transport Made Simple group, and buses are being branded as Central Connect. Subsequent fleet investment has seen the arrival of new Alexander Dennis Enviro200 MMCs and Enviro400 MMCs. Services link Diss with Norwich, Bury St Edmunds, Bungay, Beccles, Eye and Ipswich. Despite indications to the contrary, one of the new Enviro200 MMCs, 367 (YY24 HBL), is arriving in Diss on service 112 from Eye, having started in Ipswich on service 114. Transport Made Simple has since acquired Konectbus from Go-Ahead.

In the past couple of years, Thetford-based Coach Services has refreshed and expanded its network of services from Thetford to King's Lynn, Norwich, Bury St Edmunds, Brandon, Mildenhall and Attleborough, and invested in new MCV EvoRa-bodied Volvo B8RLEs and Alexander Dennis Enviro400 MMCs. The Breckland Beeline service 90 linking Thetford and Attleborough with Norwich via the A11 was introduced in December 2023, as illustrated by route-branded Enviro400 MMC CS73 BUS loading in Thetford.

Dews of Somersham operates routes across Cambridgeshire, serving Ely, March, Chatteris, Ramsey, St Ives, Cambridge, Huntingdon and Peterborough. The bus fleet consists mostly of secondhand Volvos and Scanias, supplemented by five MCV EvoRa-bodied Volvo B8RLEs purchased new. Pictured arriving in St Ives on service 301 from Ramsey is newly-acquired V200 DEW, a Scania OmniCity new to London United as YP59 OEN.

First Bus Eastern Counties services along the coast from Martham in Norfolk down to Southwold in Suffolk are branded as Coastal Clipper and worked by 12 Wright Eclipse Gemini-bodied Volvo B9TLs in this blue livery. Six similar Cabriolet open-toppers operate the seasonal 1C service from Hemsby Beach to Great Yarmouth, as illustrated by 37067 (CRZ 488), new to First West Yorkshire as YK57 EZW.

Nowadays Fowlers of Holbeach Drove only runs two bus services, the 43 from Sutton St James to Spalding four times a week (Monday, Tuesday, Wednesday, Friday) and the 43A from Sutton St James to Wisbech once a week (Thursday). Just arrived in Spalding is BX56 XBU, a Wright Eclipse Urban-bodied Volvo B7RLE. Route branding has been applied to the livery it wore when with National Express West Midlands.

The Lynx network in west Norfolk radiates from its base in King's Lynn to Hunstanton, Fakenham, Wisbech and Downham Market. Twenty Optare Tempos have been joined by four new Alexander Dennis Enviro200 MMCs, and seven Enviro400 MMCs have been bought new since 2021. One of these, 64 (YX72 OLO), is in Hunstanton working the Coastliner service 36 from Fakenham via Wells-next-the-Sea to King's Lynn.

Award-winning Sanders Services of Holt continues to invest heavily in its bus operations, which stretch from Norwich north to the coast, and link Cromer with Great Yarmouth. At Wells-next-the-Sea, its Coasthopper service meets the Coastliner service of Lynx. Over 20 MCV EvoRa-bodied Volvo B8RLEs are now operated, and new double-deckers include three Alexander Dennis Enviro400 MMCs and three MCV EvoSeti-bodied Volvo B8Ls. One of the latter, 127 (ED23 SAN), is seen arriving in Cromer on service X44 from Sheringham to Aylsham and Norwich.

Ixworth-based Mulleys Motorways is the dominant operator in Bury St Edmunds, with town services and routes to Mildenhall and Newmarket. Ipswich is also reached from Hiltcham and Bildeston. The newest vehicles in its mixed fleet are two rare diesel-engined Optare Metrodeckers from a cancelled Reading Buses order. This is one of the pair, YJ23 EKN, departing Bury St Edmunds on service 355 to Mildenhall.

Whippet, now part of the Ascendal group that also owns Hong Kong Citybus, runs services connecting Huntingdon, St Neots and Cambridge. In addition, two cross-city services funded by the University of Cambridge are operated, linking Eddington to the north with the Biomedical Campus to the south, and using the guided busway. Nine Mellor Sigma 12 electric single-deckers, manufactured by Wisdom Motor in China, were purchased to work the routes, the only examples built for the UK, and these are destined to remain unique as Mellor has ceased to import them. The offside guide wheel is clearly visible on WG115 (MX73 GBY) as it makes a turn on the U1 in Cambridge city centre.

There's a tale to tell

CHRIS DREW explains the story behind a selection of photographs he took in London Transport territory between 1968 and 2011

Great Transport Extravaganza

One of the briefs held by the commercial photographer I worked for in the 1970s was Castrol Oil. In November 1974, my employer Kingston Photographic was asked to take the publicity shots of the 75th anniversary stand in the National Hall, Olympia for the Great Transport Extravaganza.

We had to get there several hours before the doors opened, so it was an early start from our office in Richmond. The boss's Austin A40 was packed to the roof with floodlights, a camera box filled with a couple of 5x4 bodies with several lenses for every occasion. Two dozen double darks with various films loaded and the usual huge wooden tripod that wouldn't move for anything less than a direct hit in a Zeppelin raid. To finish the ensemble, a couple of Weston meters which would have to agree with each other before the job could start.

As the trainee, I lugged the equipment through the hall

from the car park, but I couldn't help but notice a couple of buses parked at one end.

The shoot took twice as long as it should have and by the time we finished, the public were being let in to the hall, so we had to clear up quickly. On the promise of a coffee and a sticky bun, Mr John gave me 5min to get my photographs of the buses.

During the official shoot, I had been eyeing up possible places to take my photos. I ran up a set of temporary stairs and found a gap in the stalls on the balcony. I had to hold my breath to keep the camera still and this shot was the outcome. Nearest the camera was K424 which had been brought from the London Transport Museum at Syon Park for the occasion. I never did get the number of the DMS, appropriate really, I suppose because as a group, they were quite anonymous.

'I don't want a black and white Cadillac car'
Marc Bolan 30/9/47 - 16/9/77

The irony is, if he had been in a large car he might have got away with it.

Marc Bolan (born Mark Feld) was best known as the front man of Tyrannosaurus Rex the psychedelic folk duo who later shortened its name to T Rex and with the release of the single *Ride a White Swan* headed off into Glam Rock fame. In the early 1970s, sales of T Rex records (vinyl) accounted for 6% of total sales in Britain.

The next few years saw them guesting with Ringo Starr, Elton John and Ike and Tina Turner and moving to America. As with most bands when one member is more charismatic than the rest, the line up began to disintegrate and by the mid 1970s Marc Bolan headed off for a solo career.

On the night of the September 16, 1977, he was a passenger in purple Mini being driven by Gloria Jones as they headed for his home on the Upper Richmond Road in Sheen, south-west London. As the car was crossing the railway bridge at Queen's Ride on Barnes Common, she lost control and struck a sycamore tree. Bolan was killed instantly. Within a short time, it became a focal point visited regularly by followers of the band who placed fresh flowers and photographs at the site. On what would have been his 60th birthday in 2007, it was recognised as Bolan's Rock Shrine.

As for the irony at the top of the page, Bolan never learnt to drive because he had a morbid fear of dying young in a car crash. He did, though, own several cars. One of which, a Rolls-Royce, was the one he should have been in that night, but his management had lent it to the band Hawkwind and the rest as they say... His ashes were interned at Golders Green cemetery.

At the time and to the best of my knowledge, Queen's Ride has never been part of a bus route. This all changed for a few weeks in March 2011 when the realignment of the railway bridge at Barnes station meant one-way working going north. Routes 33, 72 and 265 travelling south had to follow a diversion which, for the 33 and 72, meant going once around the route 22 terminus loop on Putney Common to get them pointing in the correct direction. As one can guess, I took several photographs in the time the diversion was working because how was I to know if it would ever happen again? That, I suppose, is how history works.

Black Shadow to SuperBus

Stevenage new town? There has been a centre of population at Stevenage since Roman times. It rests close to the road from Verulanium to Baldock. Stithen ac, one of its names in old English, means 'place of the strong oak'.

The modern age of Stevenage began after World War Two with the Abercrombie Plan. This called for a ring of new towns around London. Stevenage was given the first. The local population were not keen on being taken over by a concrete jungle. The protesters renamed the plans 'Silkingrad' after the minister in the Attlee government who pushed it through against their wishes. The Old Town was supposed to be left untouched, but the town hall was knocked down as a symbol that power was being taken away from the previous inhabitants.

Stevenage was the manufacturing site for what was then the world's fastest production road motorbike, the Black Shadow. Built by Vincent HRD Motorcycle Company, it had a — all but 2cc — 1litre engine which was an integral part of the strength of the bike instead of being a dead weight resting on the chassis. It gained its name because everything was finished in black, even the crankcase and covers giving it a sleek look not seen before.

Twenty years later and along came a bus, also in colours not normally associated with a utility vehicle, on to the streets of Stevenage in December 1969. Those streets which, because the planners wanted to keep transport and pedestrians apart except for specific places, were wide, straight and with roundabouts instead of traffic

lights. This meant a new type of bus service was needed. The crew-operated RT not only looked lost in the scenery but presented an image not conducive to a modern town.

In the last month of London Transport ownership, the Country Area placed three XF Fleetlines in service. They were borrowed from East Grinstead garage and painted blue and silver. The name Blue Arrow was chosen for the pre-booked, home-to-work service operated at peak times.

They weren't the greatest success, but they were a toe in the water. The following year, a Better Buses for Stevenage demonstration was arranged with two SM-class AEC Swifts and two Metro-Scanias, one from Leicester, the other a demonstrator, shown to the public as a possible way to go.

Blue Arrow did not to last much longer, but it spurred on into being, the SuperBus idea. The canary yellow and Oxford blue made the service stand out from the crowd. The fleet ended up with a mixture of Swifts, Metro-Scanias and Leyland Nationals and from the photograph of SM499, we can see that the staff at Stevenage garage were not the best at keeping these buses clean, negating the special feel of the service.

By the end of the decade, the SuperBus name was gone in favour of StevenageBus and National Bus Company green. Move on to the end of the first decade of the 21st century and up and down the country, bus companies are waking up to the fact that the SuperBus style of service was a good idea.

Waterloo Sunset, Autumn 79

It was a sad way for a relationship to end.

The saga had started on April 18, 1966, when a skinny youth made his way to Victoria with a pocket full of tanners. I took my place in the queue and soon a gleaming steed arrived, and the line slowly began to disappear inside it. Like a bunch of schoolchildren waiting at the tuck shop, we all held our shiny sixpences tight in our sweaty hands in case it would leap out and run away, leaving the owner with the embarrassment of rummaging through his pockets to replace it.

This was the day that Londoners were introduced to the concept of the Red Arrow bus with route 500 taking to the road.

Then it came to my turn. I shuffled past the driver as I tentatively moved towards the turnstiles. I chose the left one, found the slot for my tanner, waited for it to drop, then pushed hard against the milk stool-shaped turnstile. Now, when I said that I was skinny, I was, as my dad would say, a 'rasher'. I needed help from the chap behind me to get through. After that, there was a cavernous dance floor of an area to stake a claim in. Standing was not thought popular by London's travelling public, but this was the dawn of a new era, very continental, so chic. Café culture was just around the corner.

The 500 was a short express-style route running between Victoria and Marble Arch by two routes depending on the time of day, with only one other stop at Hyde Park Corner. As with many political decisions about transport, if the project, at first sight, was considered a success, the whole system had to change.

More Red Arrow routes would come into existence and high-capacity single-deckers would be the order of the day. It soon got back to the research and development teams that they had not done the jobs they were paid for. In places the vehicles were too large for the garages, the rigours of London work meant there were many failures and maintenance costs were higher than the older rear loader. Except for the Red Arrow routes where they broke all the rules and flourished.

A nucleus was kept after the rest had been withdrawn. Over time the gadgets disappeared. The turnstiles and change machines ended up as so much rusty scrap metal and the driver took over the job of collecting the cash or checking passes.

As I travelled, I saw turnstiles jam, change-giving machines give up and refuse to hand over the loot. I also spent the rest of the day learning to find the sweet spot on the turnstiles so as to not embarrass myself anymore. Little over a decade and a half later, I would be around to see their downfall.

MBS544 was one of my regular steeds and was seen working the 503 in the autumn of 1979. There was only a little time to go before it was withdrawn and in 1981, that version of the route. This left the 507 as the only Red Arrow route between the two points. It was seen leaving Westminster Bridge Road and entering the tunnels which gave a dramatic entrance to Waterloo station.

A huge thanks to Raymond Douglas Davies for the title and the music...it's a pity that nobody was around to iron out the kinks.

The Ladies Bridge

Of all the millions of journeys made across Waterloo Bridge each year, how many ever stop and think about the history of the bridge they're standing on?

The first bridge to carry the name was opened in 1817 and a toll was charged to cross it. It was built of granite and designed with nine arches of 120ft each separated by double Doric stone columns. It gained the rather sorry reputation for being a good place to commit suicide. A poet of the day, Thomas Hood wrote a piece called *The Bridge of Sighs* which made account of the number of prostitutes who ended their lives jumping from the parapets.

The downfall of the original bridge was started by the demolition of the Old London Bridge. After it was taken away, the river flowed with greater speed, and the stonework piers of the old bridge began to scour and subside to such a point that by the 1920s it had to be shut for major strengthening as it was in danger of collapse.

By this time, the London County Council said enough was enough and commissioned a new bridge to replace it. Designs were drawn up by Sir Giles Gilbert Scott. Scott by his own admission was not an engineer, so he hired Ernest Buckton and John Cuerel who worked for the engineering company of Rendel, Palmer & Tritton to solve the problems.

Part of the bridge was open for use by March 1942 and completed by the end of the war in 1945. It also was the only bridge on the Thames to sustain damage by German bombers.

Still to this day parts of the story of the bridge remain a mystery. At the beginning of the war when the Irish labourers went home, their jobs were taken by women. As with many industries, women filled the positions vacated when the men were called up for active service. There is precious little, if any, paperwork still in existence about this because when the building contractor Peter Lind & Company went into receivership, the documents about the project were destroyed. There have been moves over the past few years to try and uncover more details about the women who built the bridge. Their legacy is kept alive though because boatmen who give trips to tourists still refer to Waterloo Bridge as The Ladies Bridge

This photograph took the best part of 3hr to get which I won't get back. I prefer to think of it as dedication rather than 'Get a life'. DMS2641 gives tourists the views they paid to see while DM1707 potters along the embankment mostly empty on route 109.

It's all his fault

When I left primary school at the age of 11, I, along with my classmates each received a leaving present. In the preceding few weeks, teachers had been quietly gaining information to make that present a useful one for the child in the future. It was at this time that the stirrings of my hobby were beginning so I was given...a bus book.

It was called *The London Bus & Tram Album* and had a large colour photograph of a Routemaster on the dustcover. It was edited by someone whose name kept cropping up all through the years of my hobby. That name? VH Darling.

It was filled from end to end with a cornucopia of photographs and information that opened a new world to me. It took some time and lots of re-reads for it to sink into my memory but once it was there, it stayed. This is why my frontal lobes fizzed into action when I saw RM494. Let me explain.

On p33 of the book, there's a photograph of G251, a Massey bodied Guy Arab II. It was taken by DWK Jones and the text that went with it stated that the bus was 'unique in having no trace of cream relief anywhere'.

Move forward to the summer of 1968 and while walking from Victoria station to Gillingham Street garage I caught sight of RM494. It took a second glance to realise that it didn't have a cream band round the middle. Was history repeating itself? Was this another unique bus? I grabbed the camera but was annoyed that I couldn't get a clear shot. Over the years my opinion of it has changed and now I wouldn't have had it any other way.

Later I was to find out that RM494 was one of half a dozen similar Routemasters working the 127 from Highgate garage as an experiment, one that didn't go any farther at the time but reappeared under the privatised schemes nearer to the end of the Routemaster era.

Also later, I found out that VH Darling was not who she was reported to be and if you're able to read this in an afterlife, Michael Dryhurst, you now know it's all your fault.

Colchester Corporation was one of the 57 municipal fleets that Massey supplied, the Essex undertaking purchasing 55 double-deck bodies between 1939 and 1968. In the centre of this line-up is 34 (MWC 134), one of seven 7ft 6in-wide Leyland Titan PD2A/31s new in 1963. Its final Massey bodies were ten square profile 74-seat ones on its first rear-engined buses, Leyland Atlantean PDR1/1s. Nearest the camera is 46 (WEV 746F) from the initial batch built in late 1967, while 50 (AVX 50G) on the left was the first of a final quintet new in autumn 1968.

A Massey market

MICHAEL DRYHURST pays photographic tribute to a Lancashire bodybuilder whose customers extended across the length and breadth of Great Britain

Although the one-time frontrunners of British bus bodybuilding were the likes of Eastern Coach Works (ECW), Metro-Cammell, Park Royal, Weymann and Alexander, the second tier offered some notable companies such as East Lancashire Coachbuilders (better known as East Lancs), Northern Counties, Charles H Roe and...Massey Bros.

It was in 1904 that brothers William, Isaac and Thomas Massey formed their business of timber merchant and building contractor in Pemberton, a parish a couple of miles west of Wigan town centre.

Of the latter activity, the company constructed houses, schools, mills and even cinemas. In 1919 it added the building of vehicle bodies, for cars and vans; bus bodywork came later, in the early 1920s, double-deckers

before the end of that decade. As Massey double-deck bodywork became increasingly popular it was to be found eventually on motorbus chassis built by AEC, Bristol, Daimler, Foden, Guy and Leyland.

What made this company stand out was its customer base, which stretched from the north of Scotland to eastern England and East Anglia, including much of the north of England, to the valleys of south Wales and operators in north Wales, to the south-western peninsula and even the island of Jersey.

Among these were many municipal operators, but Massey products were popular also with those independents that bought new buses rather than used hand-me-downs. During World War Two it was one of nine bodybuilders enlisted to produce the austerity utility

Massey built the 32-seat rear-entrance single-deck bodies on five Leyland TB3 trolleybuses supplied in 1936 to the Tees-side Railless Traction Board. They were withdrawn prematurely in 1944 when modifications to the overhead under a steel works railway bridge allowed the board to introduce its first double-deck trolleybuses. They were sold to North's of Leeds, a prominent dealer in secondhand buses, which sold them to Southend Corporation, which ran them until around 1952. Southend 142 (VN 9437) was TRTB's no.12. DEREK GILES/THE BUS ARCHIVE

The fascinating Massey-bodied Leyland TB10 'low-loading' trolleybus. It was tested on the South Lancashire Transport system but never went into production. LEYLAND

double-deck body, building it on Guy Arab I and II, Daimler CWG5 and CWA6 chassis with design features that made them instantly recognisable.

Among the wartime Guys were 49 for London Transport, the only Massey bodies it bought. A wartime shortage of many paint pigments meant that all 49 were delivered in a brown livery; all but one were based at Enfield garage.

Perhaps the most interesting double-decker that Massey ever produced was the body for the Leyland experimental TB10 trolleybus chassis. This was a tri-axle unit, known as the 'low-loader', for which the Wigan company produced a

lowheight H34/29D body, with open platform and enclosed front door, ahead of the front axle. Leyland built many of the bodies on its own chassis until 1954, so it is perhaps surprising that it did not build this one, too.

It was an exhibit at the 1935 Commercial Motor Show in London. It could be said the bus was doomed from the start, as all trolleybuses available then were built on modified motorbus chassis, while the custom-built TB10 would have been considerably more expensive. It was inspected by London Transport but never trialled in service there, at a time when it was initiating a huge programme to convert the north London tram routes, involving over 1,500 trolleybuses, most of them Leylands.

Massey was not the only player in its home town. There was the Northern Counties Motor & Engineering Company, which although based in Wigan was owned by a Welsh family, which accounted for its registered address being in Cardiff. Until 1942, the future Welsh capital (it only gained that status in 1955) purchased many bodies from Northern Counties, including its first trolleybuses, the only such buses the company bodied. By contrast, Massey built 69 trolleybus bodies between 1935 and 1942.

The housebuilding and construction activities of Massey lasted until 1962, the sole pursuit thereafter being bus bodywork including its first rear-engined double-decker, a Daimler Fleetline in 1964, but Northern Counties acquired the company and its factory in March 1967. Among the Massey products delivered after the takeover was the last lowbridge side sunken gangway double-decker built, a Leyland Titan PD3/4 supplied to Bedwas & Machen UDC in June 1968. It is one of a significant number of Massey products that, fortunately, survive in preservation. ∎

Images enhanced by ALASTAIR BATESON

The last trolleybus body produced by Massey was in 1938, of updated styling and fitted to Ipswich 86 (PV 6426), on a locally-built Ransomes, Sims & Jefferies chassis.

The Massey wartime austerity body was possibly the most angular of all the World War Two utility bodies, and most were allocated to municipal fleets, such as Coventry 322 (EKV 822), a Daimler CWG5 new in March 1943 and rebuilt by the operator in 1951.

Merthyr Tydfil Corporation 8 (HB 6264), a Massey-bodied Bristol K6G new in July 1947 and extensively rebuilt in 1952.

Sunderland Corporation 99 (GR 9931), a Daimler CVG6 new in July 1948, carried a Massey body incorporating immediate prewar styling with subsequent early postwar look. The glazing was not shaped but the metal sheeting above it was.

This view of Stockton Corporation 49 (KPT 754), a 1949 Leyland Titan PD2/3, shows the rear-end treatment of the initial post-World War Two Massey double-deck body.

Massey's northernmost customer was Aberdeenshire operator James Sutherland (Peterhead) Ltd, which purchased two AEC Regent IIIs in 1949 with lowbridge bodies. They exchanged Sutherland's red and cream livery for the blue and cream of W Alexander & Sons when taken into state ownership in 1950 and gained the yellow and cream of Alexander (Northern) after the Scottish Bus Group's largest subsidiary was divided in three in 1961. FAV 827 was Alexander's RC22 when photographed in Aberdeen in May 1959. It survives in preservation.

The East Anglia municipals all favoured Massey bodywork. Reminiscent of tramway practice is the fleetname on this Lowestoft Corporation 28 (LBJ 743), one of a pair of crash gearbox AEC Regent IIIs new in 1951.

Newcastle Corporation bought 52 Massey bodies, 28 of them in 1948/49 on AEC Regent IIIs including 101 (LVK 101).

This Foden PVD6, 7 (XRE 590), was purchased new by WS Rowbotham of Harriseahead, Staffordshire in 1952. Potteries Motor Traction acquired the independent in 1959 and operated the Foden for several years.

In 1961, Massey gained a new customer, Jersey Motor Transport, for whom it built ten 40-seat single-deck bodies on Leyland Tiger Cub chassis. These were shortened to cope with the island's difficult road system.
CHRIS DREW COLLECTION

Essex independent Moore Bros. of Kelvedon bought 67-seat lowbridge Massey bodies on six 30ft long Guy Arab IV chassis between 1958 and 1961. They passed into Eastern National ownership when it took over Moore's business in 1963, and by 1981 this one was in California, painted in London red and owned by a pub in Burbank; it ended its days in a breakers' yard in Las Vegas.

It should be no surprise that Wigan Corporation, serving Massey's home town, was its third largest customer after Birkenhead and Bolton, taking 102 bodies between 1920 and 1968. Forward-entrance Leyland Titan PD2/37 139 (DEK 2D), with the later square profile body that was more utilitarian than elegant, was one of a pair new in 1966. Now preserved, it was photographed back in Wigan depot in 2011, then used by First Manchester and today by Go North West.
NORMAN PRICE

Massey built the last lowbridge side sunken gangway body in the UK in 1968. This was Bedwas & Machen 6 (PAX 466F), a 68-seat Leyland Titan PD3/4 now preserved.
RICHARD FIELD

South Yorkshire's rocky ride to deregulation

MIKE GREENWOOD, information officer at South Yorkshire PTE when bus services were deregulated in 1986, provides a photographic journey from 1984 to 1988, illustrating the build-up to D-Day and the early years of the new environment

The radical years of South Yorkshire's grand design for public transport began with the creation of South Yorkshire PTE and South Yorkshire County Council in 1974 through to bus deregulation in October 1986. This is an era still remembered for its cheap bus fares policy, but there was a lot more to it than that.

The policy on fares was not to put them up. For eight years they were frozen and with high inflation this meant that they became ever cheaper in real terms. Eventually a point would have come when it would cost more to collect the fares than charge them. At that point bus travel would have become free.

The policy was very popular locally with more than a million people signing a petition to keep the policy in place. It was also effective in keeping bus patronage high — even to increase it — and road congestion low, with traffic congestion in Sheffield lower than in any comparable city.

However, it was not a popular policy in Whitehall or Westminster, and not just with Margaret Thatcher's Conservatives. James Callaghan's preceding Labour government also did its best to try to get the PTE to see the error of its ways although the Conservatives delivered the fatal blow which started in 1984 with a proposal to deregulate local bus services.

This was published in a White Paper, Buses, and Part 1 of the Transport Act 1985 brought these proposals into effect. This eventually led to fares going up by up to 300% in one day. Bus patronage decline and traffic congestion were the inevitable consequences. ∎

The bus industry showed its opposition to the deregulation of local bus services on November 27, 1984 with a parade of buses driving past the Houses of Parliament.

I drove SYPTE's Travelling Promotion and Information Bus from Sheffield to London which seemed to take forever thanks to its restricted top speed. BWB 148H was a Park Royal-bodied Leyland Atlantean PDR2/1 new to Sheffield Joint Omnibus Committee in 1969.

This picture was taken at the assembly point in London, next to HWJ 693J, South Yorkshire County Council's Park Royal-bodied Daimler Fleetline CRG6LXB campaign bus, which had been new to Sheffield Transport in 1971.

Making up the South Yorkshire trio was brand new PTE Dennis Dominator 2358 (B358 CDT) with Alexander lookalike body built by East Lancs. In the parade were buses from Chesterfield, Darlington, Edinburgh, Hartlepool, Hull, Merseyside, Tyne & Wear, Nottingham and Tayside.

There also were bus parades in other towns, and this was part of the procession around Doncaster on December 1, 1984.

Before joining SYPTE, I worked for Leicester City Transport and on two occasions it was arranged for me to bring buses to South Yorkshire from Leicester. On the second occasion I requested one of the three East Lancs-bodied Dominators which were part of a vehicle swap between SYPTE and Leicester before delivery.

This was Leicester 84 (B84 MRY), delivered in November 1984 and part of the same batch as SYPTE 2358 in the previous photo. In exchange, SYPTE received three new Plaxton Paramount-bodied Dennis Dorchester coaches from Leicester.

The other two buses in the photograph are a Chesterfield Daimler Fleetline and an SYPTE Metrobus in the Bus & Coach Council's nationwide 'We'd all miss the bus' campaign livery.

Despite many protests, the Transport Act 1985 was to be implemented in the autumn of 1986. The exact date was still being argued over in the House of Lords, but SYPTE saw that the writing was on the wall and started to plan for its future in the late spring of 1985.

Livery trials were carried out on Alexander-bodied Dominator 2194 (NKU 194X) which used a pinkish cream called Cameo together with a skirt in chestnut, a shade of brown, as seen on May 17, 1985. This looked a bit too close to the original PTE livery and if the new arm's length company was going to succeed in a competitive market it needed a bolder, more distinctive identity. Advertising agencies were invited to pitch for a complete rebrand.

The winning agency came up with a livery adding poppy red to the Cameo and chestnut colours. Wrapping the whole package together was a new slogan 'SYT around South Yorkshire'. This enforced the South Yorkshire Transport's brand and played on SYT being interpreted as 'sit'. A completely new symbol, with interlocking letters S, Y and T, was also designed.

The first bus in the new livery was Dennis Dominator 2189 (NKU 189X), seen on publicity duties on September 18, 1985.

Deregulation may have been inescapable, but the Fight to Save Your Service campaign bus, in use since November 1984, continued to tour the region inviting the public to sign a petition to save their service. Here is WWJ 771M, a Park Royal-bodied Fleetline new to Sheffield Transport in 1973, in Sheffield city centre on October 14, 1985.

Buses repainted from late summer of 1985 received a Cameo and chestnut scheme in readiness for completion once the new livery was finalised.

This is 523 (FHL 523V), one of two East Lancs-bodied Dominators ordered by Doncaster independent Morgan and Store but delivered to SYPTE in May 1980, following the independent's acquisition, in Haymarket, Sheffield on October 14, 1985.

Once the new SYT livery was agreed, poppy red was added to buses which had received the Cameo and chestnut base along with subsequent full repaints.

Among the older types in the new livery was 1511 (OKW 511R), a 1977 MCW-bodied Leyland Fleetline FE30 which resembled London Transport's DMS class. It was in Sheffield's Pond Street bus station on November 8, 1985, standing out from similar 1512 behind in SYPTE livery.

SYPTE was one of the first operators to promote access to the network for older and disabled people through concessionary fares and with some buses adapted to carry wheelchair users. Among the latter was 65 (KKW 65P), a 1976 Alexander-bodied Leyland Leopard PSU3C/4R with a wheelchair lift added to the rear in 1986 and painted into Coachline livery to appeal to a broader market. This shows it in Sheffield on June 30, 1986.

Competition against SYT came in all shapes and sizes from new small start-ups to large existing companies. Representing the latter was the West Riding Group, based in Wakefield, which had the former Sheffield United Tours garage in Charlotte Road already on its books and used it as a base for a new company called Sheffield & District.

It tendered successfully for schools services as well as main ones abandoned by SYT. To rub salt in the wounds, its Charlotte Road garage was directly opposite SYT's East Bank garage.

A former Yorkshire Traction 1973 Leyland National became S&D 95 (NHE 407M) and the ECW-bodied Leyland Atlantean AN68A/1R on the right, new to Yorkshire Woollen in 1979, became S&D 764 (JYG 419V). This photographed at Charlotte Road premises on November 11, 1986 also shows green and white buses in the background ready for further expansion.

Another new bus operator to enter the fray in spring 1987 was SUT, owned by the ATL Group, which also ran out of the Charlotte Road premises.

ATL had purchased NTE Coaches in the National Bus Company privatisation programme, a company that had once been the old respected Sheffield United Tours coaching business. ATL sold off the coaches which it had acquired but was unable to use the Sheffield United Tours name for its new planned bus operation because that name was now owned by Wallace Arnold. The name would not have been appropriate anyway for a bus operation and the letters SUT were used.

The livery application was similar to that of Sheffield & District but with maroon rather than blue. The initial fleet was gathered from far and wide and included this 1976 ECW-bodied Daimler Fleetline CRG6, 40 (JOX 440P), one of a pair ordered by Harper Brothers of Heath Hayes but delivered to Midland Red. I photographed it on September 13, 1987 at a Transport Rally on Norfolk Park in Sheffield.

SYT closed its East Bank garage in Sheffield as an economy measure in April 1988. Four months later, most of the East Bank management team went into business as Yorkshire Terrier which soon became a thriving and successful business. It started up with seven secondhand Leyland Nationals, including 3 (LMO 227L), a former Alder Valley example new in 1973, photographed in High Street, Sheffield on a service 16 journey to Crookes.

Established Sheffield independent coach operator Richardson's Travel made successful tendered service bids from the outset in October 1986. It also started new commercial services from the Dearne towns to Sheffield and Doncaster using ex-NBC Leyland Leopards.

This was the company's yard on August 6, 1988 with a variety of rolling stock ready for action, all turned out in an attractive livery. There are AEC Reliances and Leyland Leopards with Plaxton Panorama Elite, Plaxton Supreme and Willowbrook 003 coach bodies, Plaxton Derwent and Duple Dominant bus bodies. Former owners include Crosville, London Country, Lancashire United and Mayne of Manchester.

Still life scenes

Frustrated by a technical advance that spoils photography of moving vehicles, **TONY WILSON** seeks out locations where they can be captured standing still

Many modern electronic destination displays frustrate photographers, as much of the information is either blurred, broken up or missing altogether owing to the constant refreshing of modern day digital and other forms of display technology.

This occurs especially when attempting to capture a vehicle on the move but can also occur when stationary. To counter this, adjustments to the speed of the camera's exposure are necessary to something like 1/125th of a second or slower. Gone are the days of boards and roller blinds, hence photographers' habits have had to change to achieve the desired result of a vehicle complete with its information clear and intact.

I prefer nearside shots — another photographer nicknamed me Nearside because of this — without the clutter of street furniture and foliage. Naturally these would be captured in motion around 1/300th or faster.

I now try to capture either very slow moving or — better still — stationary vehicles. Thus, a busy bus stop is probably my ideal location, which set me thinking what I had from my archives that would fit the bill from days gone by. ∎

To set the modern scene, Norfolk-based Sanders Services 543 (KF74 SAN), one of a growing number of Volvo B8RLE with MCV EvoRa bodywork in its fleet. When paused at a stop in Holt town centre in March 2025, the clear digital destination display captured at 1/100th of a second. The clock was not part of the bus stop, merely the result of my position in the road, something I realised only after taking the picture.

There were no such photographic concerns 55 years earlier in 1970 when destination blinds were printed on fabric. This also was on the north Norfolk coast, at Mundesley, where Eastern Counties 663 (NAH 663F), a Bedford VAM5 with ECW body, was parked and the driver was outside, studying the fulsome timetable on the bus. The shape of the windscreen and grille gave these buses a rather sad look with drooping eyes and open mouth.

What better way is there to experience the Lake District than from upstairs on an open-top double-decker? Passengers were doing just that in May 1995 as Leyland Atlantean 1928 (ERV 251D) in the Stagecoach Cumberland fleet pulled away from the bus stop on Stock Lane, Grasmere. New in 1966 to Portsmouth Corporation, its Metro-Cammell body had its roof removed for further employment on the tourist trail.

Local government reorganisation turned Accrington Corporation into Hyndburn Borough Council in 1974. Its buses were kept in their traditional dark blue and red, which were later refreshed with light grey, as illustrated in June 1995 by 49 (GCK 49W), a Leyland Leopard with East Lancs body built in nearby Blackburn. The bus shelter alongside is in the same colours.

When the new Pavements shopping centre was completed in Chesterfield during 1980, semi-covered bus stops were incorporated on the north side of New Beetwell Street, providing limited protection against the prevailing weather conditions from the south. The then Prince and Princess of Wales officially opened the centre in 1981. The part covered stops are behind Chesterfield Transport 155 (UWA 155S), a 1978 Leyland Fleetline with Roe bodywork, in July 1996.

Robin Hood Airport, opened in 2005 on the site of the 90-year-old RAF Finningley air base, was soon renamed Doncaster Sheffield Airport. Several bus routes were created or extended to serve it, one of the new ones being the 707 direct from Doncaster, operated by Wilfreda Beehive with YJ05 XOO, an Optare Tempo in overall advertising livery. A bus stop was placed conveniently outside the main terminal building. The airport closed in November 2022 but is expected to reopen in 2027.

The Harrogate Bus Company upgraded its flagship route 36 (Leeds-Harrogate-Ripon) in 2025 with new generation Alexander Dennis Enviro400EV electric double-deckers. These replaced the Wright Gemini 3-bodied Volvo B5TLs that had served the fleet for the previous seven years. This March 2024 picture shows one of them, 3641 (BF67 GOE), departing from the moss-covered southbound bus shelter in Ripley village, between Ripon and Harrogate.

With a healthy loading of passengers in June 2024, Southern Vectis 1524 (HW62 CNU), an Alexander Dennis Enviro400, had just pulled away from the westbound bus stop of route 12 from Newport that served the Mottistone National Trust property on the Isle of Wight. A 1/125th exposure speed was required otherwise the Alum Bay destination would have been illegible. The bus stop complements the Southern Vectis livery.

After Lincolnshire and Eastern Counties, Crosville was the largest operator of the ECW-bodied Bristol SC4LK, building up a fleet of 79 between 1957 and 1961. The company retained SSG612 (782 EFM), new in 1957, as an operational heritage vehicle after it ended its days as a Busway maintenance vehicle at Runcorn depot and restored it at its central works in Sealand Road, Chester, to original condition with fleetnumber SC12, as seen in Owain Glyndwr Street, Aberystwyth in July 1983.

Cambrian excursions

JOHN WHITEING takes a nostalgic journey through parts of north Wales

North Wales, lying north of a line drawn roughly between Aberystwyth and the English town of Shrewsbury, is a land of mountains and valleys where beautiful scenery draws many holidaymakers.

There are other attractions for those so-minded in the area's heritage railways, both the world-famous narrow-gauge lines such as the Talyllyn and Ffestiniog and revived standard gauge lines such as the Llangollen Railway.

Added to these are the many seaside towns on the north-western coast including Llandudno, Colwyn Bay and Rhyl and resorts along the shore of Cardigan Bay like Aberystwyth.

The geography dictates that main roads, and therefore bus routes, particularly in the more rugged areas, follow the valleys containing much of the urban settlement. Many of the more local services operating to the smaller villages run on market days only, reflecting the sparse passenger base.

These photographs, arranged in chronological order, give a flavour of some of the vehicles operating there between 1983 and 2002. ■

One of many Wrexham area independents at the time, Chaloner of Moss started operating buses in 1929. It remained a one-bus operation for most of its existence and never exceeded three. This Willowbrook-bodied Bedford SB5 (PCA 331P) was purchased new in 1976 and was sold for scrap in 1992. This June 1985 picture was taken in Mold Road as it headed out of Wrexham past the football ground. The business continued to operate the same service to Moss and Summerhill from Wrexham until April 2003 when GHA Coaches took over the bus (by then a Mercedes-Benz 811D) and service.

ER Pritchard, trading as Purple Motors of Bethesda, was one of countless independents to buy ex-London Transport Daimler Fleetlines in the early 1980s. Park Royal-bodied MLK 670L (formerly DMS670 and new in 1973) heads out of Bangor along Beach Road on the Bangor-Bethesda service in April 1988.

Crosville Cymru had two of these Optare Delta-bodied DAF SB220s. In July 1989, five months old SDD702 (F702 ECC) has just reversed into Station Road in the village of Llanuwchllyn, at the south-western end of Llyn Tegid/ Bala Lake and headquarters of the Bala Lake Railway, while operating service 94 from Wrexham to Barmouth/ Abermaw. The move was necessary to allow buses to continue their journey in either direction along the main road.

Within the port of Holyhead in September 1990 on a shuttle service for B+I Line is OR Jones's Leyland National NPK 235R, new to London Country in 1976. This was the first to join the fleet, earlier that year, and wears Jones's fleet livery. Around a dozen followed, many for port-side shuttles in blue and white B&I livery, which this one subsequently did. Jones has been in business since 1936 and still operates today, based in the Anglesey village of Llanfaethlu around ten miles from Holyhead.

Goodsir of Holyhead HRE 531N, an ECW-bodied Bristol VRT/SL2 new to PMT in 1975 and acquired from there in 1990, had a Bws Gwynedd red front applied to its fleet livery when photographed near Holyhead station in August 1991. This operator also continues to trade and currently operates five services in the Holyhead area including service 24 to Morawelon on which the VR was operating.

Bryn Melyn Motor Services of Llangollen operated a few double-deckers from time to time although the fleet at the time of this photograph in Market Street, Llangollen in August 1999 was principally single-deck and minibus. F201 EPD was a Dennis Dominator with East Lancs bodywork to semi-coach specification new to London & Country in 1989 and acquired in 1998. GHA Coaches acquired Bryn Melyn in 2007 and operated it as a distinct unit until 2015. GHA ceased trading the following year.

Based at Abermule, an out-station of Shrewsbury, Midland Red North 1730 (YPJ 207Y) was an ex-Alder Valley Leyland Tiger coach new in 1983 with a Plaxton Paramount body liveried for the Reading-Heathrow RailAir Link. It was sold to Midland Red North in 1991 and rebodied by East Lancs. When photographed in Welshpool in August 1999, it was in the operator's retro livery. It was operating the lengthy D75 service from Shrewsbury to Llanidloes, part of the Bws Powys network. Until 1971 this service was operated by Mid Wales Motorways and subsequently by Crosville and Midland Red, the latter retaining Crosville's route number. Those who knew and loved Midland Red in its heyday will recall that its D-prefixed routes were Dudley local services.

Jurassic Coaster-branded First Hampshire & Dorset 33970 (SN65 ZDG), an Alexander Dennis Enviro400 MMC, arriving in Portesham on the X53 service to Weymouth.

Far from the Madding Crowd

BOB HIND samples the bus routes of rural Dorset in pursuit of the inspiration for the works of novelist Thomas Hardy

Most routes in Dorset would make a scenic league, hence the county's attraction to writers and poets. The landscape and history are full of characters and stories and while the Jurassic Coast attracts pre-history enthusiasts, I am exploring the quieter areas where its most famous writer lived.

Thomas Hardy was born in 1860 in the village of Higher Brockhampton, eldest child of a master mason. He apprenticed as an architect and practised in London for five years, but returned to Dorchester where, over 25 years, he wrote 14 novels and over 50 short stories. His novels were meticulously detailed and his characters complex, but it is easy to identify locations, which although given fictional names, attract followers nearly 200 years after these stories were published.

I am starting in Poole, leaving by Go South Coast's Morebus service X8 aboard an original model Alexander Dennis Enviro400. This runs hourly between Poole and Blandford, a small Georgian town on the River Stour.

Poole bus station is packed and chaotic. Although there are staff dedicated to reversing vehicles off their stands, I marvel that there seem to be few accidents. Poole also has, and Morebus considers important, a staffed enquiry office and a comprehensive network booklet.

The X8 leaves promptly at 12:50; our driver seems to know everyone who boards, "C'mon Brian, we haven't got all day". We skirt Poole Harbour towards the A35. A common feature on this trip will be thatched cottages and picturesque villages. Our first stop, Sturminster, has stocks on the green.

After a quick diversion into Tesco, we are in the centre of Blandford on time at 13:28. This market town was virtually destroyed by fire in 1731 but owes much of its fine Georgian architecture to that unfortunate event.

My trip into Hardy's Country begins in earnest at 14:05 with the Damory (another Go South Coast business) service CR9 for Dorchester, the heart of Hardy's fiction. The CR9, financially supported by Dorset County Council, runs three journeys a day on weekdays. It needs the

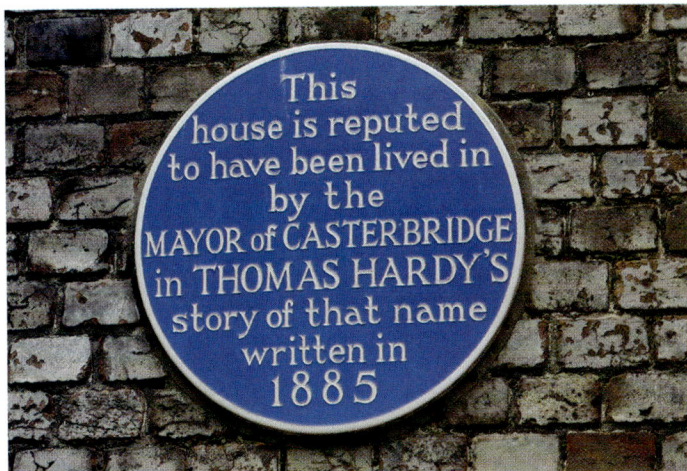

A self-explanatory blue plaque at Barclays Bank in Dorchester.

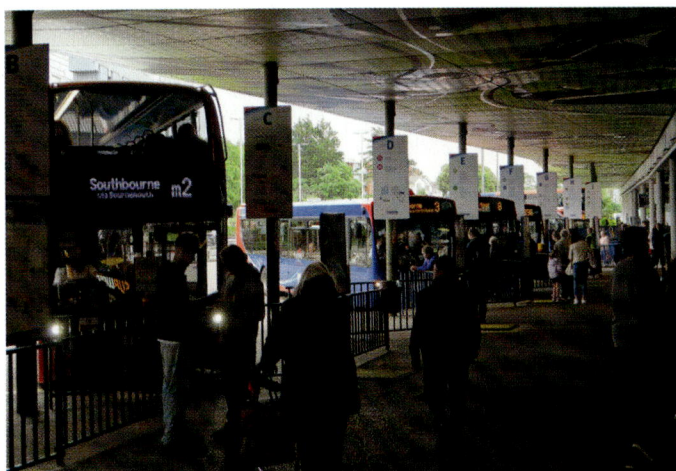

The concourse at Poole bus station with a choice of Morebus services.

support as, for half the journey, I am alone aboard the Alexander Dennis Enviro200.

Hardy adopted the historical name of Wessex for what he described as his own 'partly real, partly dream country'. Bere Regis (known to bus enthusiasts for the erstwhile operator of that name) became Kingsbere-sub-Greenhill in *Far from the Madding Crowd* and boasted its annual sheep fair as 'the busiest, merriest, noisiest' of them all. It could not be more of a contrast today: I see no one along its narrow village street.

The CR9 now does a circle linking, often by single track roads, three Puddle villages — Briantspuddle, Affpuddle and the most historically significant, Tolpuddle with its museum commemorating the Martyrs condemned to transportation to Australia in 1834 for the 'felony' of forming a union against the tyranny of landowners.

The larger village of Puddletown (Weatherby in the novels) was home to Hardy's grandparents and was celebrated for its music tradition in *Under the Greenwood Tree*. The unfortunate Fanny Robbins in *Far from the Madding Crowd* was buried here.

Casterbridge and the chalk giant

Stinsford, that we pass as we get close to Dorchester along the A35, is Mellstock in *Under the Greenwood Tree*. It is as close as we will get to Hardy's birthplace in Higher Brockhampton as there are no bus services there despite the National Trust now owning Hardy's Cottage.

Our approach to Dorchester, the county town, is possibly better known by its fictional name, Casterbridge, as many local businesses have considered it beneficial marketing to use the name.

Damory-liveried Go South Coast 2767 (YX17 NHV), a 39-seat Alexander Dennis Enviro200 new to Thamesdown, outside the Crown Hotel in Blandford on service CR9.

South West Coaches YG58 PGZ, an Optare Solo M880 new to Dorset County Council, loading in Trinity Street, Dorchester on service CR5A to Yeovil.

The Mayor of Casterbridge is considered one of Hardy's finest works. Barclays Bank in South Street is reputed to be the location for Mayor Henchard's house. St Peter's Church, The King's Arms Hotel, The Corn Exchange and the Antelope hotel all appear in his novels. A statue of the author sits at the Top O' Town on the western approach and Max Gate, also owned by the National Trust, where Hardy lived for over 40 years, stands on the eastern side of town.

I venture north on the subsidised CR5A. South West Coaches runs five weekday journeys between Dorchester and Yeovil. The 16:00 Optare Solo from Trinity Street is quite busy, and we experience the Dorchester afternoon peak. We divert into an industrial estate and queue to exit, exacerbated by roadworks and slow-moving traffic. It takes 30min to leave Dorchester behind and return to a more familiar Dorset landscape.

We weave through pretty Charminster and climb to Charlton Down. The place has a strange feeling. The central building, Herrison Hall, was opened as an asylum in 1863 and although the hospital closed in 1992 and has been converted into apartments, it still looks like a Victorian hospital.

It's drizzling and there is low mist on the hills so, as we enter Cerne Abbas, we cannot see its most famous landmark. Hardy called it Abbot's Cernel and based the Great Barn in *Far from the Madding Crowd* on the tithe barn in the village. But the 180ft hillside chalk giant will always bring visitors here.

Rolling hills, woodland and narrow lanes lead us to Sherborne which is Sheraton Abbas in *The Woodlanders*. The historic market town sits on the River Yeo with an abbey founded in 705AD and two castles, one the ruins of a 12th century fortress, the second a 16th century mansion.

We join the fast-moving A30 for the final dash towards Yeovil, but I leave at one of the town's two stations, Pen Mill, as the only way back to Dorchester, while tasting more of Hardy's countryside, is by GWR's Heart of Wessex railway.

The little halts of Yetminster, Chetnole and Maiden Newton are as near as you get by public transport to Melbury Osmond, Melbury Bubb and Eversholt. The Melburys feature in *The Woodlanders* as Great, Kings and Little Hinstock, Evershot becomes Evershead in *Tess of the d'Urbervilles*. I reach Dorchester in the early evening. It's quieter now but looks a little tired and run down. A couple of miles away I will discover a complete contrast.

An artist's impression

The first Jurassic Coaster X51 to Bridport and Axminster,

Portland Coaster-branded First Hampshire & Dorset 32031 (OIG 6947), an open-top Alexander ALX400-bodied Volvo B7TL new in Southampton in 2000 as W801 EOW, operating service X52 at Bridport bus station

operated by First Bus, leaves Dorchester South railway station at 07:53. I walk through the town centre on a beautifully sunny morning. It is market day, as it has been since Hardy's day, and the stalls are in full swing opposite the Brewery Square retail development.

The driver tells me she started out from Weymouth at 05:45 to Bridport before returning to Dorchester. She says, jokingly, that she has had a lie-in; yesterday she started at 05:15.

We leave punctually and pass Hardy's statue and the Victorian barracks, now a museum, at The Keep as we leave along Bridport Road. The X51 runs two hourly from Weymouth through Dorchester and on to Axminster. Within 10min we are at Poundbury which I can only describe as an artist's, rather than a town planner's, vision of what a new town should be. The buildings are bright Portland stone, the open space, the squares are designed to impress and consider pedestrians a priority to traffic. The building began in 1993, and the final phase should complete in 2028. It is beautiful contrast to Dorchester.

We are soon back on quiet country lanes through Winterbourne Abbas with warnings of crossing ducks. When we regain the A35 there is a warning that this area is prone to fog. We have climbed into the open with

a panoramic view showing the Channel to the left, the endless green landscape of the Dorset countryside to the right and the distant Wootton Hills.

We reach Bridport at 08:40. It is market day here as well and the stallholders are busy in the morning sunshine. I leave the X51 in the bus station next to the small First Bus depot. People are already gathering for destinations east and west on the Jurassic Coaster.

Hardy uses Bridport, long renowned for its rope and net-making industry, as Port Bredy for his story *Fellow Townsmen*. The Town Hall, St Mary's Church, The Bull's Head and the local industries all feature in the novel.

Harris and the thatchers

I find First's Weymouth and Jurassic Coaster guide in the information office as I have not seen any on buses and return to the bus station for the 09:30 X52 to Weymouth. The X53 joins the X51 to form an hourly summer frequency between Bridport and Axminster and the X52 joins in to provide the hourly coastal route between Bridport and Weymouth when the X51 leaves for Dorchester.

So, there are three Coasters loading around 09:30 and a service heading inland to Beaminster and Yeovil. My X52 is confusingly a Portland Coaster open-top — an

A 2021 picture of First Hampshire & Dorset 33707 (SN12 AHU), an Alexander Dennis Enviro400, passing through Abbotsbury — famed for its swannery — on service X53. Bob Hind covered that section on the open-top X52.
RICHARD GODFREY

Alexander ALX400-bodied Volvo B7TL built in 2000 — but my fellow passengers are excited to sit in the open air. I opt for cover near the front. We head for the seafront at West Bay where the marina and 18th century West Bay Hotel make a colourful scene.

At Freshwater Beach Holiday Park, a dozen passengers and an electric wheelchair are squashed into the hedgerow — there is no footpath. A family joins me at the front; the youngest, a boy about five named Harris, asks where the seatbelts are but is excitedly distracted when he sees their caravan from the upper deck.

In Burton Bradstock thatchers are replacing a roof, "They're building a house of straw," says Harris. It's a slow ascent as the land falls away to the beach, but in the distance is a misty Portland Bill, and then a spectacular view of Chesil Beach stretching out below us.

In picture-postcard Abbotsbury, its main street lined with beautiful stone cottages, most of them thatched, an acute narrow left turn proves troublesome for the six cars that must reverse to allow our bus access.

At 10:16, I leave the X52 at Portesham, a village that claims two Thomas Hardys. The author, whose character Bob Loveday in *The Trumpet Major* visited 'Pos'ham' to ask the other Hardy if he could serve on HMS *Victory*. That Hardy, Admiral Sir Thomas Masterman Hardy, an earlier distant relative of the author, lived here until 1807. He is best remembered as Captain Hardy who was at Nelson's deathbed at the Battle of Trafalgar. Portesham is celebrating 1,000 years since it appeared in the first Anglo-Saxon written charter of its boundaries. So much history for one small village.

The 11:17 X53 will continue my journey to Weymouth with further glimpses of Chesil Beach from a Jurassic Coaster-branded Enviro400 MMC. Our arrival at 11:45 is a dramatic change to the country scenes we have encountered earlier. Weymouth is awash with holidaymakers, in the town, on the beach, surrounding Punch and Judy. The King's Statue in the middle of the bus terminus a reminder that Weymouth has been a celebrated resort for centuries. George III visited 14 times from 1789.

Hardy worked here in 1869 when the architect firm he worked for in Dorchester was bought out by a Weymouth

The view north from the Olympic Rings sculpture on Portland Heights.

company. As the fictitious Budmouth Regis, *Under the Greenwood Tree* was written here and the location also appears in *The Return of the Native*.

The Olympics and two lighthouses

My final Hardy location visit requires a ride on the open-top Portland Coaster, another of the same batch of ALX400-bodied Volvos. In high season it runs hourly but there are just four a day today. I join a dozen hardy souls on the top deck; it's still breezy as we set off at 12:40. Our destination, the Isle of Portland, became the Isle of Slingers in *The Well Beloved*. The inspiration for the heroine's cottage now houses the Portland Museum.

We leave the town and the marina crossing over the estuary on the Town Bridge and, after a steep climb, drop down to the Portland Beach causeway past the sailing academy and numerous windsurfers. As we climb again, we pass Portland Castle, built by Henry VIII in the 1540s to protect England from French and Spanish invasion.

Higher up, Chesil Beach disappears into the distance. Even higher, in front of the Portland Heights Hotel, is the

sculpture of the Olympic Rings carved into Portland Stone to commemorate the 2012 Olympics when Weymouth hosted sailing and windsurfing events.

As we near Southwell, we are blocked by workmen. Our driver asks if we want to walk the remaining couple of miles to Portland Bill while they rebuild the road. They are only spreading tarmac, and we are soon on our way.

Our journey ends at Portland Bill where there are two lighthouses. The older one, first lit in 1716, was replaced in 1906. My plan is to return to Weymouth by the Dorset County Council community bus back to Castletown, then local service 1 which runs every 10 to 18min depending on the time of day (as there are normally four journeys in each hour, why can't it be every 15min?). The community bus does not appear, so I make most of the walk back that the Coaster driver had joked about earlier.

No one needs an excuse to visit Dorset. It is one of the UK's most picturesque counties, but to revisit the 19th century country folk and their stories, through the eyes of a renowned novelist and poet, is another reason entirely. ∎

JCY988 is a Plaxton Excalibur-bodied Dennis Javelin new in 1996 to Paramount Coaches of Mosta and still running there, passing the Valetta war memorial. It was one of three delivered at the time to Paramount. Most Excalibur bodies were built on Volvo B10M chassis and only around 20 of the 3.5m high design were produced on Javelins.

Malta coaches in the 2020s

Do you still pine for the eccentric old route buses of the Mediterranean island? **DAVID LONGBOTTOM** suggests you turn to the resident coaches which include repatriated examples from the UK and types unique to the island state.

Since the traditional Malta route buses bowed out in 2011 many enthusiasts are less interested in operations there, but the coach fleets of Malta, and neighbouring Gozo, still have much to offer for those with an eye for vehicles familiar in the UK.

There are around 200 full-size coaches operating there and around 80% of these have been sourced pre-owned from the UK or Ireland.

Historically, coaches were referred to in Malta as unscheduled buses. Indeed, it wasn't until the 1980s that imported coaches were allowed to enter service as they arrived, rather than being rebodied. The mid-1990s saw around 30 brand new vehicles being delivered, including ten unique-to-Malta Irizar Century-bodied Volvo B10Ms, Scanias bodied by Egyptian coachbuilder Ghabbour, Unicar-bodied ERF Trailblazers and Plaxton Excalibur-bodied Dennis Javelins.

Many of those are still operating, although coming to the end of their days as legislation prohibits coaches

operating once they reach 35 years of age. Modern coaches on Malta will have no difficulty reaching that age thanks to their relatively low mileages — the island is only 17miles by 9miles at its largest points — and legendary high maintenance standards.

There has been no repeat of large numbers of new vehicles being sourced, the vast majority being used, although a notable exception was in late 2023 when four electric Yutong coaches arrived, the first for the island.

In addition to the Volvos and Scanias being imported, around a dozen former National Holidays Setras were purchased and there is a growing number of Temsas.

There are operators of long standing, and some have formed cooperatives which give the impression of a larger concern. The KopTaCo cooperative combines at least a dozen operators in a corporate brand and livery, while the UCS (Unscheduled Coach Services) consortium members' vehicles wear their own livery and branding with supplementary UCS lettering.

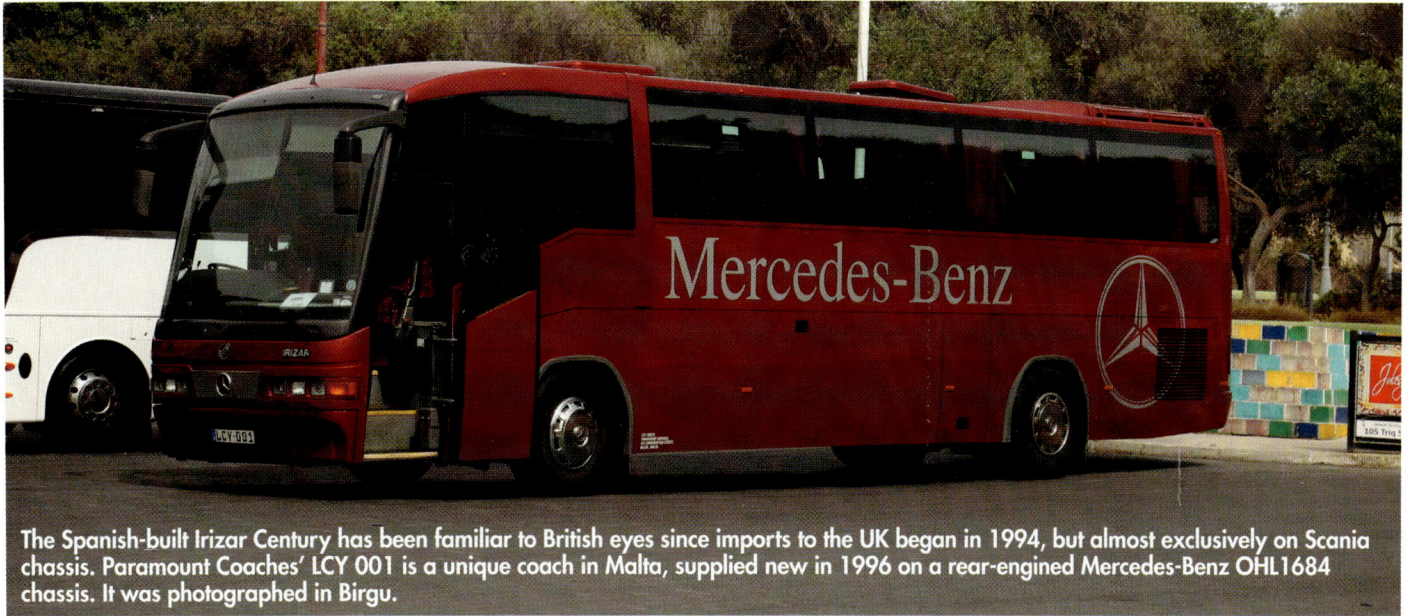

The Spanish-built Irizar Century has been familiar to British eyes since imports to the UK began in 1994, but almost exclusively on Scania chassis. Paramount Coaches' LCY 001 is a unique coach in Malta, supplied new in 1996 on a rear-engined Mercedes-Benz OHL1684 chassis. It was photographed in Birgu.

Larger independent operators such as Paramount, Supreme and Zarb are familiar sights throughout the island.

There are just over 40 coaches on Gozo, with many operators part of the Gozo Coaches cooperative. As on Malta, while newer vehicles are arriving, Dennis Javelins were common until recently, including the last operational Duple-bodied coach on the islands. There are still around half a dozen examples of the Maltese built coach, the Scarnif-bodied Optimal.

If you visit Malta and you happen to sip on a glass of Cisk and sample the local cuisine at a pavement café and think that coach passing by looks familiar, it may well have worked for your local operator back home. ∎

Supreme Coaches ACY971 is one of ten unique-to-Malta Irizar Century-bodied right-hand-drive Volvo B10Ms new in 1995, photographed passing the harbour at Spinola Bay.

Built mainly for South Africa, five ERF Trailblazer coaches were supplied new to Malta in 1995. LCY983 was one of four with Unicar bodywork and, when seen in 2024 at the Sicily ferry terminal at Marsa, was the last of its type still operational. It was working for Silverstar, with UCS branding in the windscreen.

FBY073 is the last operational Duple coach on the Maltese islands. The Duple 320 Express-bodied Dennis Javelin was new to Bebb Travel of Llantwit Fardre in 1988 as E32 SBO and was exported in 1999. It operates with Zomber Travel and was parked outside its home garage on the edge of Victoria, the principal city on Gozo, wearing Gozo Coaches Co-operative livery.

This UCS-branded coach passing through Sliema, BPY685, one of the few survivors of the eight Egyptian-built Ghabbour-bodied Scania K93s delivered new in 1995.

Supreme Travel BCY 924 climbing the hill at Spinola Bay with mix of modern and traditional Maltese architecture behind, together with an Otokar route bus. The Plaxton Premiere 350-bodied Volvo B10M-62 was new to Wallace Arnold as R435 FWT in 1998 and reached Supreme Travel in 2003 after spending a year with Vale of Llangollen Travel in north Wales.

The Citadel in Victoria towers above Gozo Coaches-liveried FBY070, a 1998 Maltese-built Optimal with Scarnif coachwork.

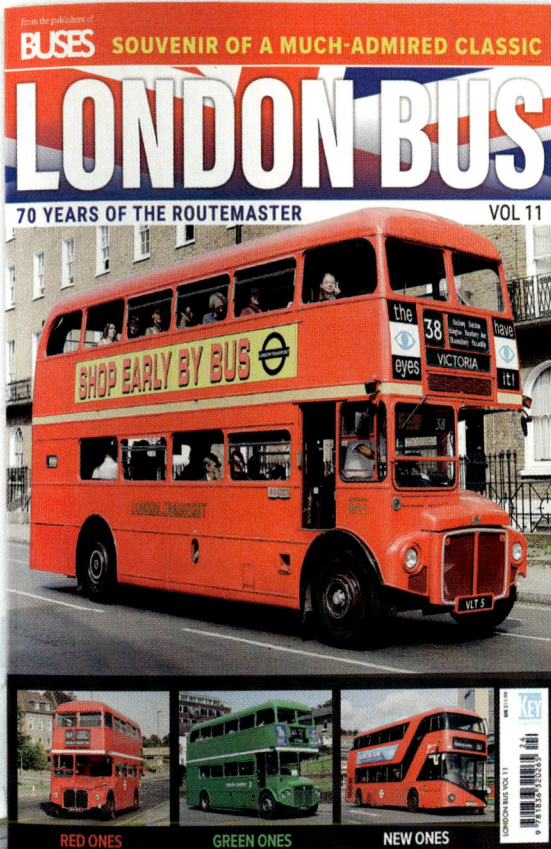

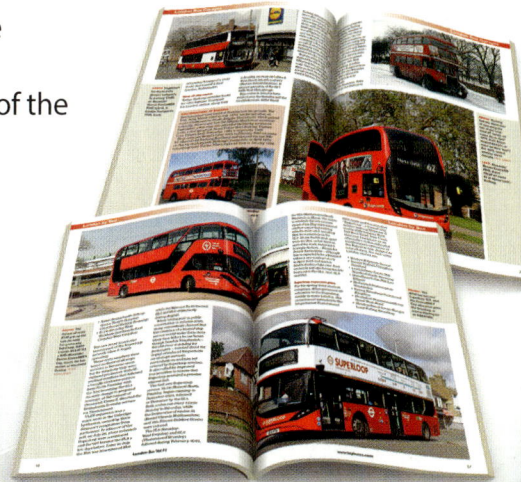

Water buses in Beds

DANIEL STAZICKER finds a ford for two rural routes to negotiate

The small central Bedfordshire village of Sutton, 11miles east of Bedford and close to Potton, is one of the few places in Britain where buses run regularly through a significant ford with water flowing. Alongside the ford is a 13th century packhorse bridge made from local sandstone, which gives pedestrians a dry crossing point.

Sutton has a population of around 300 who benefit from two local bus routes. Grand Palmer operates route 190 (Blunham-Sandy-Potton-Biggleswade) every 2hr on Mondays to Saturdays, shown here with 8.9m Alexander Dennis Enviro200 MMC 231 (YX71 OJF).

East Beds Community bus supplements it every Thursday with its Ivel Sprinter minibus providing one return journey into St Neots, with 2hr for shopping, on its 193 (Biggleswade-St Neots) round trip. Its Iveco Daily, BX17 XCA, has a proper bus-type destination display. ■

130